Creative Groups Guide

Blessed Are We

13 Complete Lessons

Adapted for Group Study by Jan Johnson

STANDARD
PUBLISHING
Cincinnati, Ohio

Creative Groups Guide: Blessed Are We

By Jan Johnson

Edited by Dawn B. Korth
Cover design by Barry Ridge Graphic Design

The Standard Publishing Company, Cincinnati, Ohio.
A division of Standex International Corporation.

05 04 03 02 01 00 99 98   5 4 3 2 1

ISBN 0-7847-0750-2

$\mathcal{C}$ontents

*I*ntroduction

Welcome to Creative Groups Guides!

Whether your group meets in a classroom at the church building or in the family room in someone's home, this guide will help you get the most out of your session.

You can use this Creative Groups Guide with or without *Blessed Are We*, the companion book written by LeRoy Lawson. Use this guide even if you haven't read that book. But if you do read it, you'll be even more equipped for leading the group.

Each section in this guide includes two plans—one for classes and one for small groups. This gives the leader several options:

• Use the plan just as it is written. If you teach an adult Sunday school or an elective class, use Plan One. If you lead a small group, use Plan Two.

• Perhaps you teach a Sunday school class that prefers a small group style of teaching. Use the discussion questions and activities in Plan Two, but don't overlook the great ideas presented in Plan One. Mix and match the two plans to suit your class.

• Use the best of both plans. Perhaps you could start off your class with a discussion activity in Plan Two, and then use the Bible-study section in Plan One. Use the accountability, worship, or memory verse options presented in Plan Two in your Sunday school class. Use some of the "Sunday school" activities and resource sheets presented in Plan One in your small group meeting. Variety is the spice of life!

Resource sheets in each session are available for you to tear out and photocopy for your class or group. Overhead transparency masters are also included for most sessions. Use your own creativity as you decide how to make these resources work for you.

This guide has been developed to help you do several things. First, you'll be able to facilitate active and interactive learning. These methods help students remember and put into practice what they learn. Second, you'll help your class or group apply the lessons to their lives. These sessions will help your group members actually do something with what they're studying. Third, we've given you lots of options. Only you know what will work best in your class or group. Finally, support and encouragement are integrated into each session. Learning and application happen best when participants are helping one another. That may mean accountability if your group has built up the trust and caring it takes, or it may simply mean that people are lovingly encouraging one another to continue growing in knowledge and action.

How to Use This Guide

Each session begins with an excerpt from *Blessed Are We*. This excerpt summarizes the session at a glance. Use it in your preparation or read it to your class or group as an introduction to a session. The central theme and lesson aims help you understand the main ideas being presented and what outcomes you are looking for.

Materials you might need on hand to conduct your session are listed on the first page of each of the plans.

In both plans, there are three main parts to each session: Building Community, a warm-up activity or icebreaker question; Considering Scripture, Bible-study activities and discussion; and Taking the Next Step, activities or discussion that will help participants apply what they have learned.

In Plan One for classes, the names of activities are listed in the margins, along with the suggested time for each one. Use these as you plan your lesson and as you teach to stay on track. In most cases, optional activities are listed. Use these instead of or in addition to other activities as time allows.

A number of options are included in Plan Two for groups. Use the accountability-partner option to help the group support, encourage, and hold one another accountable. This works particularly well in a group in which trust has already been gained between participants. Accountability partners can help one another put what they are learning each week into practice. They can pray with and for each other throughout the week. They can "spur one another on toward love and good deeds" (Hebrews 10:24).

Other options include worship ideas and a memory verse. Use these at your discretion to help your group grow in love, devotion, and praise for God and for hiding his Word in their hearts.

Use this guide to help you prepare, but we suggest that you do not take this book to your class or group meeting and merely read from it. Instead, take notes on a separate sheet of paper and use that as you lead your group.

One

Before the Blessing Comes the Prioritizing

But seek first his kingdom and his righteousness, and all these things will be given to you as well. Therefore do not worry about tomorrow, for tomorrow will worry about itself. Each day has enough trouble of its own" (Matthew 6:33, 34). You'd think that Matthew 6:25-34 would be called the Great Beatitude. For most of us, nothing sounds more blessed than to be free from worry. But before the blessing comes the prioritizing, remember?

We begin thinking about our priorities as children. What do I want to be when I grow up? Or do? Or have? These questions don't go away when we become adults. I was still asking them in my forties. For that matter, now that my contemporaries are racing into retirement, they've come back again with a vengeance. What do I want to do with my remaining years? Shall I preach, shall I teach, shall I try for things beyond my reach?

—LeRoy Lawson, *Blessed Are We*

Central Theme	To seek God means to let God stretch us, letting His priorities become our priorities.
Lesson Aim	Group members will look at a biblical example of how Jesus stretched people and consider how we can be stretched to align ourselves with God's priorities.
Bible Background	Matthew 6:33; Luke 5:1-11
For Further Study	Read Chapter 1 of *Blessed Are We*.

PLAN ONE

Classes

BUILDING COMMUNITY

Display Transparency 1 (or write the categories printed on it on the chalkboard) and ask, **Which of these activities involves the most risk to you? You may vote twice.** Ask for a show of hands for each item and keep a tally to the right of each one.

Before conducting the above survey, display Transparency 1 and ask class members to add their ideas of risky activities to the list. Then take a vote.

Ask class members as they arrive, **What is the riskiest thing you've ever done?** Be ready with your own story or a suggestion or two (see Transparency 1) to get the class going.

CONSIDERING SCRIPTURE

Ask class members to find a partner and turn to Luke 5:1-11. Distribute photocopies of Resource Sheet 1A, "You're the Director!" Then give directions such as these: **Imagine for a moment that you are the director of a movie based on this passage. Imagine also that you will be out sick for the day of the filming. Write stage instructions for the actor portraying Peter. Based on what you find in the passage, tell the actor who plays Peter what to do and what his attitude appears to be. Peter speaks only in verses 5 and 8, but he has a lot of other things to do. Write those directions to Peter in the columns on the resource sheet.**

Allow class members 5-10 minutes to work and then ask for their responses. These might include

vv. 1-4 DO: You're washing your fishing nets with other fishermen. When Jesus asks you to, row your boat out a little so Jesus can preach from it. ATTITUDE: willing and cooperative

v. 5 (Peter speaking) ATTITUDE: Speak in *protest*. We don't know if Peter said, "Because you say so" with rebellious resignation (rolling his eyes) or if he was trying to cooperate after lodging his protest.

vv. 6, 7 DO: Act quickly, yelling for the nearby fisherman. ATTITUDE: Surprised and alarmed, working hard in a crisis.

Survey
5 minutes

OPTION
Adding to the Survey
5-8 minutes

OPTION
Personal Stories
5-8 minutes

Stage Directions
10-15 minutes

Materials You'll Need For This Session

Resource Sheets 1A, 1B, Transparency 1, pens or pencils, chalk and chalkboard.

v. 8 (Peter speaking): ATTITUDE: The text doesn't give us too many clues. Perhaps Peter was fearful because he thought the sinking boat meant God was judging him through Jesus the prophet. Or, he could have been repentant for his protest.

vv. 9, 10 DO: Hold the nets, showing astonishment with wide eyes and spread hands, as if to say, *Look at this!* ATTITUDE: Incredulous, as if wondering how this could happen.

v. 11 DO: Listen to Jesus and once again become cooperative—doing the hard work of pulling a boat ashore, tying it up and leaving it (Peter probably turned it over to relatives). It's as if you're drying off your hands and going off with Jesus. ATTITUDE: Cooperative and obedient.

Continuum Evaluation
10-15 minutes

On the left side of the chalkboard, print, "cooperative/mellow." Then draw a horizontal line across the board over to the right side and print, "puzzled/overwhelmed." Have class members turn to Luke 5:1-11 and ask volunteers to take turns reading the verses. **Explain that you will stop reading five times to ask a question.** After verses 3, 5, 8, 9, 11 are read, ask, **Where on this continuum would you place Peter? Place a mark anywhere on this line.** Give the chalk to the person who has just finished reading so he or she can place a mark on the chalkboard.

OPTION
Theme Question
(3-5 minutes)

After you've finished either of the above activities, have a class member read Matthew 6:33. Explain, **This is our "beatitude" for today. It's a beatitude because those who seek God and God's priorities will be blessed with the food, drink, and clothing (vv. 25-32) they need.** Ask, **How difficult do you think it was for Peter to be stretched by Jesus and trust that Jesus would take care of him?** At times, Peter was very cooperative (lending his boat, for instance). At other times, seeking God's kingdom (doing what Jesus said) was appalling to Peter. He was afraid the loaded boat would sink. Point out that Jesus did ask Peter to risk—to take time away from work, to allow his boat to be used as a pulpit and to fish where he already had fished and failed. Finally, Jesus risked Peter's life—at least that's how it probably looked to Peter.

TAKING THE NEXT STEP

Case Studies
10 minutes

Distribute photocopies of Resource Sheet 1B, "Stretching Experiences." Ask a volunteer to read the first story. Then ask the following questions.

How did John Calvin align himself with God's priorities, even though it stretched him? By working with his friend, Farel, to further the cause of the Protestant Reformation.

How did the words of Calvin's friend, Farel, echo Matthew 6:33: "But seek first his kingdom and his righteousness, and all these things will be given to you as well"? Farel said that God wouldn't bless Calvin's plans unless Calvin cooperated with God's plans (which Farel believed were to participate in the Protestant Reformation). Calvin's devotion to his studies was not wrong, but apparently God had a different, higher priority. (Try to avoid discussions about one person telling another what God's will for them may be. In this case—and perhaps through hindsight, "Calvin heard Farel's as the voice of God, and he consented.")

How did the church member align himself with God's priorities? The man pointed out his employee's wrongdoing but gave him another chance.

What other options did this church member have as an employer? He could have fired the employee or he could have overlooked the stealing and lying.

Were these other options *wrong*? Not necessarily, but the path he chose showed he was seeking to align himself with God's priorities of compassion (giving the employee another chance) and justice (not letting the employee off the hook).

Distribute photocopies of Resource Sheet 1B, "Stretching Experiences" if you have not already done so. Read the first story again and point out the sentence that appears near the end (third to the last sentence) "But I tell you, . . ." Write this portion of the sentence on the chalkboard: ". . . because you prefer your repose to Jesus Christ." Erase the word, "repose" and ask, **What word might God put in that blank?** Give them a few minutes to ponder your question. If you wish, supply possibilities such as leisure, work, or reputation.

OPTION
Personalizing a Quote
3-5 minutes

Distribute Resource Sheet 1C, "Peter's Protests Paraphrased," and explain, **Seeking God and God's will isn't always easy. Peter protested, and even asked Jesus to get away from him. Calvin was annoyed with his friend. The member of Dr. Lawson's church took time out of his busy schedule to seek counseling about his behavior toward his employee. The key issue is to talk to God about seeking His will—even if it sounds as confusing as Peter's protests. Use the exercises on this sheet to formulate your own questions and conversation with God.**

OPTION
Peter's Protests Paraphrased
5-8 minutes

PLAN TWO — Groups

BUILDING COMMUNITY

1. At what point in your life has it been most easy for you to risk?

2. What elements need to be in place in order for you to be willing to risk—trusting the person in charge, lack of involvement of money (or children or safety)?

OPTION
Consider this cartoon (described in *Blessed Are We*):
   The man says to the pastor: "I'm tired of blessings in disguise —if it's all the same to you, I want one I can recognize immediately."

3. In what instances have you experienced "blessings in disguise"?

CONSIDERING SCRIPTURE

Read Luke 5:1-11.

1. How did Peter respond to Jesus' request to use his boat as a speaking platform?

2. What are the possible reasons Jesus might have suggested they go out to sea after he taught the crowd? (Jesus wanted to thank Peter for using his boat with a catch of fish. Jesus needed to get away from the crowd and rest.)

3. Based on the wording in verse 5, what thoughts appear to have been running through Peter's mind when he explained that they'd already fished all night and caught nothing?

4. From whom did Peter ask for help when the catch was too large? (He asked for help from his partners, James and John (v. 10). We have to wonder if he asked Jesus to help.)

5. Why does it appear that Peter asked Jesus to get away from him? (He may have been afraid, realizing Jesus was miraculous

OPTION

Accountability Partners

Have partners meet and discuss current situations in which they believe God is asking them to risk. Encourage them to listen to each other's protests (which are really to God, not to them) without judgment or advice-giving, and pray for each other.

OPTION

Worship Ideas

Read Psalm 34 together as an act of worship. Song Suggestions: "You Are My Hiding Place" by Michael Ledner; "He Will Deliver Me" by Bill Batstone.

OPTION

Memory Verse

"But seek first his kingdom and his righteousness, and all these things will be given to you as well" (Matthew 6:33).

in some way. He wanted mercy so his boat wouldn't sink. Or, perhaps Peter didn't want Jesus to go away at all, but this was an expression to communicate how unworthy Peter knew he was in Jesus' eyes—see Isaiah 6:5).

6. What was Peter afraid of (Jesus told him not to be afraid in v. 10)?

7. If you had been Peter, what would you have been afraid of?

8. How do you explain Peter moving from fear (v. 10) to obedience (v. 11)?

Read Matthew 6:33, 34.

9. What do these verses tell us about risk?

10. What do these verses tell us about priorities?

TAKING THE NEXT STEP

1. What experience in your life has been similar to Peter's trip out in the boat?

2. Did that experience have any of these elements—obeying under protest, surprises, fear, trusting obedience?

3. How has that experience equipped you for current challenges?

You're the Director!

Luke 5:1-11	what the actor playing Peter should do	the attitude he should show
vv. 1-4		
SPEAKING PART: "Master, we've worked hard all night and haven't caught anything. But because you say so, I will let down the nets." **v. 5**		
vv. 6, 7		
SPEAKING PART: "Go away from me, Lord; I am a sinful man!" **v. 8**		
vv. 9-11		

Stretching Experiences

Not only did Peter struggle with following God's priorities . . .

A much later disciple of Christ, the **Reformation leader John Calvin**, was as reluctant to take up his task as Peter is his. Guillaume Farel was importuning the brilliant but reclusive young scholar to join him in Geneva. Together, they would lead the city according to their Protestant understanding of God's will. Calvin was not easily persuaded, pleading his youth and unfitness but mainly his love for study. He was more fit for the quiet of libraries than for shouldering the onerous duties of civic leadership, for which he had no experience. Finally, according to Calvin's biographer, the exasperated Farel rose, extended his hand over Calvin, and scolded, "you have no other pretext for refusing me than the attachment which you declare you have for your studies. But I tell you, in the name of God Almighty, that *if you do not share with me the holy work in which I am engaged he will not bless your plans, because you prefer your* repose *to Jesus Christ!*" The speech may sound presumptuous to modern ears, but Calvin heard Farel's as the voice of God, and he consented. His protest was over.

One of our church members dropped by for a little counsel. His question was a big one: "How do we know the will of God?" I steeled myself for the lengthy dissertation I was about to deliver on the subject, when he narrowed the topic considerably. He didn't want general instructions; he had just come from dealing with a dishonest employee. The man had been stealing from him, then lying about his stealing. My friend has disciplined him while at the same time giving him another chance. He wanted to know whether, as a Christian trying to live by Jesus' general instructions, he had done the right thing.

. . . The dilemma his crooked employee posed for him presented itself as an excellent test case. "What would the Lord have me do right now?"

—excerpted from LeRoy Lawson, *Blessed Are We*

Peter's Protests Paraphrased

1. Consider something you think God may be asking you to do or say or change. Describe that below.

2. Consider Peter's words: "Master, we've worked hard all night and haven't caught anything. But because you say so, I will let down the nets" (Luke 5:5).

   Paraphrase Peter's words, perhaps this way:
   "Master, here's why I don't want to do what you've said" (or what I think you've said):

3. Consider Peter's words: "Go away from me, Lord; I am a sinful man!" How upset might you be if God stretched you or changed your life in some way?

   Paraphrase Peter's words, perhaps this way:
   I'm not good enough for . . .
   I'm not the right person to do this . . .
   Let me be for a while . . .

4. Consider how Peter walked off with Jesus, fully cooperating with him. What would you like to say to God about your cooperating with his priorities?

Risky Activities?

- giving a speech to co-workers ☐

- telling someone information they don't want to hear ☐

- participating in a whitewater river rafting trip ☐

- taking a job for which you have no training ☐

- meeting the person you most admire and [not?] knowing what to say ☐

- appearing on television on a talk show ☐

- seeing someone you had a fight with and haven't seen since ☐

- signing loan documents to buy a house ☐

- sending someone you love on a trip ☐

Two

What Did I Ever Do to Deserve This?

*T*he first Beatitude takes issue with a very popular, much-encouraged posture, the one that boasts, "I deserve." It assumes many forms, as in the popular lament, "What did I ever do to deserve this?" or any number of persuasive commercials, like, "You deserve a break today at McDonald's" or "It's expensive, but I'm worth it."

This "I deserve" mantra, promoted as a good exercise in building self-esteem, is as alien in spirit to the first Beatitude as it can be. Jesus reserves his praise for people who acknowledge they *don't* deserve and don't expect to be honored, or coddled, or handed good breaks, or given everything the self-satisfied are convinced should be theirs. The poor in spirit don't demand to be first in line; they don't head for the chief seats. They don't go on strike for more wages than they're worth. This Beatitude decidedly does not "Look Out for Number One."

—LeRoy Lawson, *Blessed Are We*

Central Theme	To be "poor in spirit" means to have a healthy dissatisfaction with self and possessions that makes us teachable and open to the leading of the Lord.
Lesson Aim	Group members will look at the benefits of Zacchaeus' poverty of spirit and consider ways they can become "poor in spirit."
Bible Background	Matthew 5:3; Luke 19:1-10
For Further Study	Read Chapter 2 of *Blessed Are We*.

Classes

BUILDING COMMUNITY

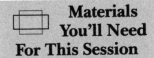

Display Transparency 2, "Down-Home Poetry," and give instructions something like this: **Let's compose a limerick using the format on this transparency. We'll write the limerick about someone who acts as if he or she knows everything. This person can be taught nothing—ever. First, let's think of some of some typical attitudes and behaviors of a know-it-all.** List these at the bottom of the transparency. After you have several, work on the limerick. See which gender most people use—man or woman—and cross out the other one on the transparency. The lines with "a" at the end all rhyme with each other. The lines with "b" at the end rhyme with each other. Use the additional room under each line for ideas that you can erase later. If you wish, photocopy Transparency 2 as a handout and distribute it to small groups to work on.

Write this sentence on the chalkboard: "I'm most likely to act like a know-it-all when . . ." Explain, **Now and then, most of us think we know more than someone else about something, and we tend to overdo it.** (Give a personal example by finishing the sentence yourself.) **Who else can finish the sentence for us?** If no one says anything for several minutes, bring up these situations: working with a new co-worker, life with children or grandchildren or nieces and nephews, playing a sport you've played for a long time, doing an outside chore that you've done many more times than you'd like.

CONSIDERING SCRIPTURE

Have a volunteer read Luke 19:1-10 and then distribute copies of Resource Sheet 2A, "A Day in the Life of Zacchaeus." Explain, **First, look at the outline of Zacchaeus's day at the top of the sheet. Look at the heading and the verses mentioned. Which details in the verses fit with the outline heading? Make a note if you wish.**

Then describe Zacchaeus's day by picking a time on the clock and inserting details about Zacchaeus's life or behavior that show his dissatisfaction with himself. Then pick another time of day and insert details that indicate Zacchaeus was

Limerick Writing
5-10 minutes

Materials You'll Need For This Session

Resource Sheets 2A, 2B, Transparency 2, pens or pencils, chalk and chalkboard.

OPTION
Sentence Completion
5-8 minutes

Clocking a Day in the Life of Zacchaeus
10-15 minutes

actively seeking Jesus. Do the same for the other two headings. You may do this activity by yourself or with a partner.

Circulate among class members, helping as needed. Then ask volunteers to show their clocks and read what they wrote. If these points aren't covered, mention them.

Dissatisfaction with self—Zacchaeus was a chief tax collector, a powerful and important person with great career success. He was also wealthy, which was significant among a conquered people such as the Jews in this time. Yet with all he had, he wanted to see Jesus even though it would be difficult to see or meet the Lord since Zacchaeus was short.

Active seeking—This important, prestigious person actually climbed a tree (a little-kid activity!) just to get a glimpse of Jesus.

Actively sought by Jesus—Jesus apparently was touched by Zacchaeus's efforts to see him and invited himself to Zacchaeus's house.

Payback time—The wealthy chief tax collector not only stopped cheating, but gave half his possessions to the poor. He would also look up everyone he cheated and make restitution four times over.

Include in your discussion the idea that this process may have taken more than a day. Undoubtedly Jesus stayed a while and worked with Zacchaeus.

Option
TV Interview
10-15 minutes

Ask class members to form pairs, and as they do so, write the four-point outline on the chalkboard (Dissatisfaction with self, Active seeking, Actively sought by Jesus, Payback time). Read today's passage together and say, **Imagine that you are a talk-show host and you're going to interview Zacchaeus. What questions would you ask Zacchaeus?** Wait a few minutes and then say, **Now, write the answers that Zacchaeus would give. Use the outline on the chalkboard to get ideas.**

Option
Acting Out the Interview
5-8 minutes

If you have time, have at least two of the pairs perform their interviews for the class. Suggest the "interviewer" start by holding up two sheets of paper and saying something such as, **We have Zacchaeus with us today. We have a copy of his bank statement from this month and last month. He has drained a great deal of money out of his account—much more than half! We're going to talk to him about that today.**

TAKING THE NEXT STEP

Thought Question
5-8 minutes

Distribute photocopies of Resource Sheet 2B, "What Does 'Poor In Spirit' Mean?" Have a few volunteers read the sheet and then ask, **In what way was Zacchaeus poor in spirit?**

Zacchaeus had that healthy dissatisfaction with himself that forced him to seek out Jesus. Once he talked with Jesus at his house, Zacchaeus was instantly obedient—giving of himself and making restitution to those he had cheated.

If you haven't already distributed photocopies of Resource Sheet 2B, "What Does 'Poor In Spirit' Mean?" and had it read aloud, do so now. Then say, **Take a few minutes to read it again to yourself. What phrases stand out—perhaps even making you think, *That's me!*? Underline those phrases.**

After a few minutes, say, **If it seems to you that God is speaking to you through any of the underlined comments on this page, place a star by those words. Perhaps you'd like to write the names of persons or situations involved in those comments. Take a few minutes to pray silently about these phrases.** (If you've already used the resource sheet with the above activity, it will still work well with this one. In fact, it will help. If they've already read the sheet once, class members will be able to identify statements more quickly.)

OPTION
"That's Me!"
(5-10 minutes)

Pick out a few songs related to the topics of poverty of spirit, teachability, seeking God, our need for God, or our nothingness without God. (Write these topics on the chalkboard, and if you wish, list the songs from Song Suggestions in the Groups Session.) Then say, **These songs deal with poverty of spirit. Let's add a verse to this song that is focused even more specifically on one of these topics or a problem area within these topics. For example, in the song, "Teach Me Lord," the word, "worship" could be changed to "seek" so that it is sung, "Teach me, Lord, to *seek* you."** Have class members form groups to do this activity, but some may want to work by themselves.

OPTION
Add a Verse
10 minutes

Some class members will like the "Add a Verse" activity, but others may not. In that case, you may wish to present both of the activities and let class members decide between them.

OPTION
Choice of Activities

PLAN TWO  **roups**

BUILDING COMMUNITY

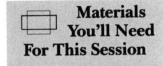
Materials You'll Need For This Session

Reproducible sheet: Resource Sheet 2B.

1. God wants us to have a teachable spirit and pliable character. What are some of the ways we behave that don't exhibit such qualities? (We are apathetic toward God; we have know-it-all attitudes; we act as if we deserve the best at all times)

2. What do you think it means to have a teachable spirit?

OPTION: If this discussion is going well, continue with:
3. Do you think that questioning yourself and what you do is a good idea? Why or why not?

CONSIDERING SCRIPTURE

Read Luke 19:1-10.

1. How would you describe Zacchaeus and his place in society?

2. Did his desire to see Jesus harmonize or conflict with his role in society? Why or why not?

3. Why wasn't it impolite for Jesus to invite himself to Zacchaeus's house?

4. Zacchaeus welcomed Jesus gladly whereas he could have been embarrassed and annoyed at having been caught in the tree. What does Zacchaeus's welcoming response indicate?

5. Jesus often shocked people by associating with the people outcast by society. What was it about Zacchaeus specifically that seems to have drawn Jesus? (See Luke 5:30-32; 15:7-10. Jesus saw himself as coming to minister to those who needed him—and *knew* they needed him! According to the way this account is written, Jesus seems to have sought out Zacchaeus not so much because he was a "sinner," but because Zacchaeus sought him.)

6. Compare Zacchaeus's response regarding his money with that of the rich young ruler (Mark 10:17-22).

Option
Accountability Partners
Have accountability partners meet and discuss more candidly their "poverty of spirit"—especially that healthy dissatisfaction with self and being open to God.

Option
Worship Ideas
Read Psalm 27 together as an act of worship. Song Suggestions: "As the Deer" by Martin Nystrom; "Thy Word" by Amy Grant and Michael W. Smith.

Option
Memory Verse
"Blessed are the poor in spirit, for theirs is the kingdom of heaven" (Matthew 5:3).

7. If you had been Zacchaeus, which would have been more difficult—parting with half of what you owned, or questioning people to find out who you cheated in order to pay back four times as much?

8. When Jesus said that salvation had come to Zacchaeus's house, was that because he promised to give away so much? Why or why not? (Good deeds don't earn salvation. Zacchaeus obviously had a seeking heart and committed himself to Christ. Christ responded to the belief Zacchaeus expressed. Zacchaeus's giving away so much was the outpouring of his new faith.)

Read Matthew 5:3.

9. In what way did Zacchaeus exemplify this Beatitude? (Even though he was rich and powerful, he submitted himself to Jesus and obeyed him in a radical way.)

TAKING THE NEXT STEP

Distribute photocopies of Resource Sheet 2B, "What Does 'Poor In Spirit' Mean?" and ask a volunteer to read it.

1. On what other occasions besides mid-life crisis do people re-evaluate who they are and what they do?

2. In what ways is questioning one's self a sign of "poverty of spirit"? In what ways is it not?

3. What are questions we can ask ourselves to maintain a poverty of spirit? (Some examples: Am I open to new ideas? Am I listening to God about my life, my relationships, my work? Do I prefer learning to teaching, listening to talking, comforting to being comforted?)

A Day in the Life of Zacchaeus

Dissatisfaction With Self (vv. 1-3)
What details in vv. 1-3 indicate Zacchaeus's dissatisfaction with himself?
With his advantages in life?

Active Seeking (v. 4)
What details in v. 4 indicate that Zacchaeus was actively seeking Jesus?

Actively Sought by Jesus (vv. 5-7)
What details in vv. 5-7 indicate Jesus actively sought Zacchaeus?

Payback Time (vv. 8-10)
What details in vv. 8-10 indicate that Zacchaeus knew what he had to do?

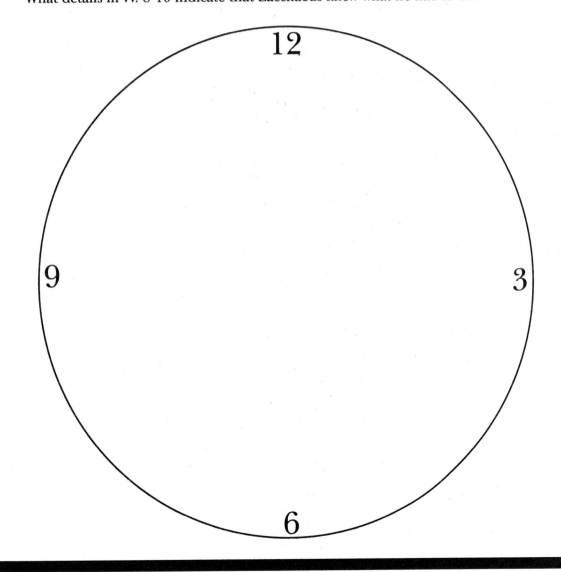

What Does "Poor in Spirit" Mean?

"Blessed are the poor in spirit, for theirs is the kingdom of heaven" (Matthew 5:3).

A Healthy Dissatisfaction With Self

As far as we know, the tax collector already enjoyed good health and lots of wealth when Jesus spied him in the sycamore-fig tree. He may have even protested that he had been obeying God, and, according to his lights, living right. By every material standard, God had treated him right. He raked in profits from the most notorious of professions. He wasn't satisfied, though. Would a complacent man have felt compelled, when Jesus came into his life, to disperse half his holdings and to repay by four times anyone he had cheated? Zacchaeus had found something (Someone?) far more satisfying than money. Suddenly, he felt the need to rearrange his priorities. He who had chased wealth would now follow Jesus.

His is not an unusual experience, especially among men and women in midlife. Scarcely a month goes by that someone doesn't seek an appointment for some career counseling. The scripts of these interviews are almost identical: "All my life I've been working to make money to buy things for myself and my family. I need a change. But I don't want to change to another job or career like the one I've got. I want to do something that makes a difference. I want some kind of ministry, where I am helping people. I want to serve the Lord."

Zacchaeus's midlife conversion leads him from dissatisfaction to liberation to peace with God in his new home in the kingdom of God.

The much-discussed midlife crisis may take many forms, but the root of the restlessness is the soul's dissatisfaction: "I don't like what I'm doing." "I'm scared my future may be nothing but more of the present." "I don't like what life has done to me." Worst of all, "I don't like the person I've become."

A Teachable Attitude

To be "poor in spirit" . . . is to be teachable, open to the leading of the Lord and willing to submit to a Savior's guidance. Some commentators believe this Beatitude to be more than the first among several; they consider it the base on which all the rest stand, serving like a heading for the others that follow. . . . If persons lack this fundamental humility, who can teach them? . . .

The "poor in spirit" don't strut, don't construct their own empires, don't delight in commanding, don't dictate others' emotions. Having found a worthy master, they are content to follow. They prefer learning to teaching, listening to talking, comforting to being comforted. They would rather see than be seen.

—excerpted from LeRoy Lawson, *Blessed Are We*

Down-Home Poetry

There once was a man/woman who knew it all,   a

Who _____ ,   a

Obnoxious as _____ ,   b

_____ ,   b

_____   a

Getting Started
typical obnoxious attitudes and
behaviors of a know-it-all

1.

2.

3.

4.

5.

6.

Three

A Time to Mourn, a Time to Laugh

*T*he second Beatitude was pretty hard for me to buy too, for a long time. It made no sense. Mourning and blessing did not belong together. After several years of pastoral ministry, though, I considered the alternative: "Blessed are those who *don't* or *can't* mourn." No, the hard-hearted or incapacitated are not blessed. They are deprived.

. . . Jesus seems to be speaking of receiving comfort *while* mourning. To all who have lost loved ones, this is good news indeed. We aren't pining to dance again; we are grateful for much less. Just a little comfort as we weep. We don't expect our sense of loss ever to leave us completely. In truth, we don't want it to. It would disappear only if we could forget our loved one, and that's a price we are unwilling to pay.

—LeRoy Lawson, *Blessed Are We*

Central Theme	Mourning is a key step in receiving comfort, which God is eager to give.
Lesson Aim	Group members look at the importance of mourning, explore issues over which we grieve, and offer a concrete expression of grief to God.
Bible Background	Matthew 5:4; Luke 18:9-14
For Further Study	Read Chapter 3 of *Blessed Are We*.

Classes

BUILDING COMMUNITY

Team Competition
10-12 minutes

Have the class members form two teams, and then offer instructions such as these: **We will go back and forth between each team until one team is unable to come up with a song that has the words, "tears" or "grief" or "crying" or "sorrow" in it. Songs can't be repeated. Country-Western songs might work especially well.** Flip a coin, if you wish, to decide which team goes first and ask that team to begin. As that team sings their song, remind the next team to prepare. Go back and forth until one team can't think of a song.

OPTION
Quote Talkback
5-8 minutes

Write this quotation on the chalkboard: "There are some men above grief and some men below it" (Emerson). Ask, **What do you think Emerson could have possibly meant by this?** Encourage class members to come up with as many different ideas as possible.

CONSIDERING SCRIPTURE

Chart Completion
12-15 minutes

Display Transparency 3, "How Was It With Their Souls?" and explain, **With the limited information we have in today's passage, let's try to monitor the condition of the souls of the two characters in this parable.**

Have someone read Luke 18:9-14 aloud (printed on the transparency) and then ask class members to help you fill in the answers.

Before the prayer—The tax collector's conscience was probably tainted because tax collectors were considered traitors to the Jews for collecting taxes for Rome. Tax collectors frequently charged more money than necessary and kept it for themselves. The Pharisee knew a lot about the law and had probably cleansed his conscience.

During the prayer—The Pharisee was thankful for his own righteousness. The tax collector was repentant.

After the prayer—The tax collector was justified in God's eyes, while the Pharisee wasn't. The humility of the tax collector would result in his being exalted. The self-righteousness of the Pharisee would result in his being humbled.

Ask this question, **How can this be—that the tax collector**

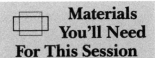

Materials You'll Need For This Session

Resource Sheets 3A, 3B, Transparency 3, pens or pencils, chalk and chalkboard.

was better off when he finished (v. 14)? God looks for a humble heart that seeks him. There is great value in mourning for our sins and the sin of the world.

Ask class members to turn to today's verse in the Beatitudes, Matthew 5:4, and read it. **How is this verse illustrated by the parable of the Pharisee and tax collector?** Those who turn to God are comforted and are then better off.

Read Luke 18:9-14 together and then have class members form two teams. Ask the first team to imagine that they are the priest who was on duty the day the Pharisee and tax collector prayed. Perhaps he overheard the prayers and was struck by how different they were. Ask this team: **What do you think you would have said at the dinner table that night to your wife?** If they're quiet for a while, say, **You might begin with, "A puzzling thing happened . . ." or, "A shocking thing happened . . .".** Then ask the other team, **Imagine you are the wife—how do you respond?** After their initial response, turn to the "priest" side again. Say, **Take the side of the Pharisee in this matter. Defend the idea that his prayer was better—after all, Pharisees and priests were often on the same political sides.** Then ask for a response from the other team, asking them to oppose the "priest-husband." Do this for several minutes until all the facts of the passage have been covered and class members have realized how appalling it was for Jesus to have elevated a tax collector over a Pharisee.

Ask class members, **What are some circumstances over which we grieve?** Urge them to help you list five or ten items in this list. After the list is made, distribute copies of Resource Sheet 3A, "Why God Grieves." Explain, **Even if we aren't experiencing bereavement, divorce, or estrangement from family** (include other items from your list), **it's important to mourn over the things that break God's heart. Two of these things are mentioned on the handout.** Have a class member read the handout.

TAKING THE NEXT STEP

Distribute photocopies of Resource Sheet 3B, "Psalm-Style Mourning and Comfort." Suggest to the group something like this: **Consider praying this psalm silently. I'll read it quietly and pause where there are brackets to give you time for thoughts of your own.**

Distribute photocopies of Resource Sheet 3B, "Psalm-Style Mourning and Comfort." Assign the lines of the psalm

---

OPTION
Mock Dinner Conversation
10-15 minutes

OPTION
Brainstorming
10 minutes

Personalizing a Psalm
5-7 minutes

OPTION
Choral Reading
5-7 minutes

printed in bold to one half of the room and the remaining lines to the other half. Choose a leader for each side. Then ask class members, **Let's read this antiphonally, with each side reading their part.** Allow some silence afterward.

Distribute paper and pencil and write this on the chalkboard: "I need to fully grieve over . . ." Encourage class members, **Finish this sentence, and as you do, write a letter to God about the things you need to mourn over and how you can anticipate God's comfort.**

OPTION
Letter to God
5-7 minutes

Groups

BUILDING COMMUNITY

1. Tell the group about a time when you fought back tears—don't be afraid to tell a funny story about choking.

2. Why do we fight tears—even when we're alone or in a movie theater when no one can see us?

OPTION:
3. It's been said there are two kinds of mourners:
- **NOW: After the event (a tragedy, a death, a divorce), they mourn openly.**
- **LATER: They don't mourn immediately after the event, but later on something (perhaps the anniversary of the event) hits them hard, and they mourn then.**
Which style of mourner are you—NOW or LATER?

4. If you can tell why you're a NOW or LATER, do so.

CONSIDERING SCRIPTURE

Read Luke 18:9-14.

1. As Jesus made up this parable, we can imagine him picking out two opposite characters: a Pharisee and a tax collector. In what ways were they opposites? in terms of faith? in terms of ethnic loyalty? in terms of religious performance?

2. The Pharisee "prayed about himself" (vs. 11). Why do we have a tendency to do that?

3. In what sense is it good to be glad you're not a robber, evildoer, or adulterer?

4. In what sense is it self-destructive to be glad you're not a robber, evildoer, or adulterer?

5. If you knew that a Christian at your place of work fasted twice a week and tithed, what would be your opinion of him or her? What does this tell you about how people viewed the Pharisee?

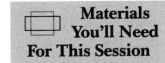
Materials You'll Need For This Session

Reproducible sheet: Transparency 3 (optional), index cards.

OPTION
Accountability Partners
Have partners meet during the week to discuss what they wrote on their index cards, even giving it to their partner if they're willing.

OPTION
Worship Ideas
Read Psalm 73 together as an act of worship, using Resource Sheet 3B, if you wish. Song Suggestions: "Mourning Into Dancing" by Tommy Walker; "It Is Well With My Soul" by Horatio G. Spafford and Philip P. Bliss.

OPTION
Memory Verse
"Blessed are those who mourn, for they will be comforted" (Matthew 5:4).

6. How could it be that a man who was a traitor to his nation (by working for the Romans collecting taxes) **and probably an embezzler as well** (charging more taxes for personal profit) **could go home justified when the disciplined Pharisee was not?** (Use Transparency 3 if you like, noting how the tax collector was the one who went away justified and was exalted.)

7. What would a sequel to this story sound like? In what way do you imagine the tax collector could have been exalted by God?

8. How did this parable speak to "some who were confident of their own righteousness and looked down on everybody else"?

Read Matthew 5:4 in several different versions.

9. In what ways are those who mourn blessed?

TAKING THE NEXT STEP

1. At what time, if any, have you mourned over your own sin as the tax collector did?

2. If you were to mourn over your sin, what sin would that be? (Be as vague as you need to be—greed, grouchiness, anger, lust.)

Distribute index cards and ask group members to number them down the side of the card from 1 to 3.

3. After number 1, write a sin of your own for which you mourn or need to mourn. Next to number 2, write an activity you do when you mourn (such as sob in the shower or dig in the garden). **Next to 3, write a way that God has comforted you in the past.**

Why God Grieves

According to the passages below, what are the reasons we grieve?

The New Testament speaks of grieving for those who show no repentance.

> Paul writes in 2 Corinthians 12:21, *"I am afraid that when I come again my God will humble me before you, and I will be grieved over many who have sinned earlier and have not repented of the impurity, sexual sin and debauchery in which they have indulged."*

Paul's heartache resonates with that of Jesus, whose ministry began with his cry from the depths. His mission was to rescue the lost sheep of Israel, but their fate was in their hands. He could deliver them only if they let him. He urgently begged them, *"The time has come. The kingdom of God is near. Repent and believe the good news!"* (Mark 1:15). The news *was* good—but their condition was deplorable. The nearness of the kingdom would be cause for rejoicing, provided they wept first.

There is a disappointment so profound it feels like mourning. For Paul, the unrepentant are like the living dead, for unless they turn their lives back to God, there is no hope for them. He looks to their future and sees only death. His mourning for them has begun.

In 1 Corinthians 5:1, 2 Paul commends grieving for the lost purity of the church:

> *It is actually reported that there is sexual immorality among you, and of a kind that does not occur even among pagans: A man has his father's wife. And you are proud! Shouldn't you rather have been filled with grief and have put out of your fellowship the man who did this?*

Some mourning is, as Charlie Brown would say, good grief.

—excerpted from *Blessed Are We*

Psalm-Style Mourning and Comfort

When my heart was grieved and my spirit embittered

(think of something that has grieved you)

I was senseless and ignorant; I was a brute beast before you.

Yet I am always with you; you hold me by my right hand.

(think of a way God has sustained you)

You guide me with your counsel,
and afterward you will take me into glory.

Whom have I in heaven but you?
And earth has nothing I desire besides you.

My flesh and my heart may fail,
but God is the strength of my heart and my portion forever.

Those who are far from you will perish;
you destroy all who are unfaithful to you.

But as for me, it is good to be near God.
I have made the Sovereign Lord my refuge;
I will tell of all your deeds.

—Psalm 73:21-28

How Was It With Their Souls?

	THE PHARISEE	THE PUBLICAN
BEFORE THE PRAYER (Base this on outward behavior and occupation.)		
DURING THE PRAYER		
AFTER THE PRAYER (vs. 14)		

To some who were confident of their own righteousness and looked down on everybody else, Jesus told this parable: "Two men went up to the temple to pray, one a Pharisee and the other a tax collector. The Pharisee stood up and prayed about himself: 'God, I thank you that I am not like other men—robbers, evildoers, adulterers—or even like this tax collector. I fast twice a week and give a tenth of all I get.'

"But the tax collector stood at a distance. He would not even look up to heaven, but beat his breast and said, 'God, have mercy on me, a sinner.'

"I tell you that this man, rather than the other, went home justified before God. For everyone who exalts himself will be humbled, and he who humbles himself will be exalted."

—Luke 18:9-14

Four

Blessed Are the Debonair

Someone recently gave me a cartoon picturing three over-stuffed businessmen at their private, linen-draped, candlelit dining table in an elegant restaurant. The very satisfied host has given his credit card to the tuxedoed waiter who holds it up, smiles and exclaims, "Ah, not merely a gold card but a gold card first class with oak-leaf cluster. How refreshing!" One guest scowls, the other looks dismayed, the host beams. His status symbol has trumped any of theirs, no doubt. In your mind's eye, try putting Jesus at the table. He'd be neither scowling, looking dismayed, nor beaming. He might be pitying, though, anyone who'd take this or any other status symbol seriously.

—LeRoy Lawson, *Blessed Are We*

Central Theme	Jesus taught that being meek means knowing what you don't know and being willing to serve others while waiting for God's assignment and reward.
Lesson Aim	Group members will look at how Jesus reversed attitudes of self-promotion, discover ways Christians can look at life as a servant and consider how God is leading them to do the same.
Bible Background	Matthew 5:5; Matthew 20:20-28
For Further Study	Read Chapter 4 of *Blessed Are We*.

Classes

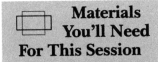

Materials You'll Need For This Session

Resource Sheets 4A, 4B, Transparency 4, pens or pencils, chalk and chalkboard.

BUILDING COMMUNITY

Display Transparency 4, "The Meek Have Already Inherited the Earth!" and read the paragraph printed on it. (Practice reading it so you read the punch line at the end well.) Then ask, **What other meek creatures have troubled you and convinced you they've inherited the earth?** Gophers in the garden are one good example. Another might be the way crying babies keep parents up at night. Try to get examples from such diverse areas as nature, corporate life, and family life. List them under "More Evidence."

Introduce this activity to class members, saying perhaps, **Name the last book you read or movie you saw that was a good example of an underdog winning freedom over a powerful enemy.** After they offer their ideas, explain this concept: **The triumph of the underdog is a common thread in good literature and is woven throughout the Bible in stories such as David and Goliath. Yet when we hear that principle in, "Blessed are the meek, for they will inherit the earth," (Matthew 5:5), the romance and drama doesn't occur to us.**

Say something like this to class members: **Tell about a time when you got into a situation where it was obvious you didn't know everything you needed to know. How did the situation turn out? Did you blunder? Did you depend on God even more?**

CONSIDERING SCRIPTURE

Distribute copies of Resource Sheet 4A, "Opposite Points of View." Help the class form two groups and assign one group the task of looking at James and John in this passage while the other group focuses on Jesus. Explain, **Answer the four questions for the characters assigned to you. Choose a recorder for your group to write down the group's answers.**

After they've had about ten minutes to work (give them a warning when only two minutes are left), ask them to share their answers with the class. Here are some possible ideas.

1. a: James and John saw a future of being like the leaders of

Exploring Meekness
3-5 minutes

OPTION
Meek Media Plots
5-7 minutes

OPTION
Group Sharing
5-8 minutes

Examining Points of View
10-15 minutes

the Gentiles—ruling over people and having authority.

b: Jesus saw a future of martyrdom and tough servanthood.

2. a: James and John thought they understood the future well.

b: Jesus knew of the future of martyrdom, but admitted that honored places weren't for him to grant, but that God would take care of it.

3. a: James and John saw leadership as a place of importance—perhaps their mother would be kneeling to them as well as to Jesus!

b: Jesus saw it as a role that required constant humility and service.

Comment that Jesus' view was radically different from that of his disciples. It's still radically different today.

OPTION
Journal Entries
15 minutes

Distribute paper and pencils and ask class members, **Imagine for a moment that you are a person interacting in this scene among Jesus, James, John, and their mother. (You might be a brother or sister to James and John—or their aunt or uncle.) Write a journal entry for that day.**

TAKING THE NEXT STEP

Group Discussion
10-15 minutes

Distribute copies of Resource Sheet 4B, "What We Don't Know," and explain, **Realizing that we don't know a lot of things is a helpful key to meekness and humility. It puts life into perspective—God knows what's going on and we're a little fuzzy about it. We are all like James and John in some ways. Let's look at those ways.** Ask a volunteer to read the sheet and then have class members form groups and explore the discussion questions below.

OPTION
Self-Evaluation Questions
10-15 minutes

Using Resource Sheet 4B, "What We Don't Know," ask class members to look at the italicized words in the statements and turn them into questions for themselves. For example, What is it I don't *understand*? That I don't *know*? That I don't *see*? Write the questions they suggest on the chalkboard and then ask them to choose one of the questions and answer it aloud.

OPTION
Prayer Prompts
2-3 minutes

Ask class members to circle the one or two items on the sheet that they need to pray about in order to let God shape them into people with a meeker spirit.

Groups

BUILDING COMMUNITY

1. What are some of the subtle things we do and say to let people know that we are really knowledgeable about a topic (sports scores, raising kids, corporate takeovers)?

2. Pick a situation in which you would like to be great—admired at work, well-known as an expert in some area. Is greatness achieved through self-promotion or through serving others? Explain.

OPTION: If your class is open about discussing their foibles, use this question:

3. If someone interviewed your spouse or best friend and asked about you, "In what situation is this person a know-it-all?" What would your spouse or friend say? (Not that their answers would be accurate, of course!)

CONSIDERING SCRIPTURE

Read Matthew 5:5 and Matthew 20:20-28.

1. What do you think it means to be "meek"?

OPTION: If you wish, distribute copies of Resource Sheet 4, "What We Don't Know." Ask the same question, but encourage group members to get ideas from the resource sheet.

2. What about James and John's mother's behavior and request tell us that she saw Jesus as an earthly ruler?

3. In what way was Jesus' reply (vs. 22) to her gracious? (In other words, what *could* he have said?)

4. SURVEY: How many of your group are surprised/not surprised that honored places in heaven are not Jesus' to grant? (vs. 23)

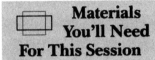

Materials You'll Need For This Session

Reproducible sheet: Resource Sheet 4B.

Accountability Partners
Have partners meet and discuss ways God is leading them to become more meek. They could also discuss questions 1 and 2 under "Taking the Next Step."

OPTION
Worship Ideas
Read Psalm 25 together as an act of worship. Song Suggestions: "Humble Thyself in the Sight of the Lord" by Bob Hudson and "I'm Forever Grateful" by Mark Altrogge.

OPTION
Memory Verse
"Whoever wants to become great among you must be your servant, and whoever wants to be first must be your slave" (Matthew 20:26, 27).

5. What are some of the reasons the other disciples might have been indignant with the two brothers?

6. Describe the Gentile style of leadership based on these phrases: "lord it over them" and "exercise authority over them."

7. Why does that style of leadership create a problem?

8. If you had been one of the disciples that day, what would have been your response to Jesus' radical statement that leadership and greatness means being a servant and slave?

9. Jesus set himself up as an example of a servant. Which account or activity of Jesus in Scripture (small or large) shows his servant's heart for others?

TAKING THE NEXT STEP

Ponder a situation in which you are a leader—in your home, at work, on the sports field, at school.

1. In what way is it easy for you to be a know-it-all in this situation?

2. In that setting, whom is God calling you to serve, or in what task is he calling you to be a servant?

OPTION: Distribute copies of Resource Sheet 4B, "What We Don't Know." After a group member reads it, re-read the first paragraph.

3. In what situation have you been asking, "Lord, will you give us what we want?"

4. When would it be convenient to spend some time praying, "Lord, what needs to be done now? What would you have us do here today?"

Opposite Points of View

Matthew 20:20-28

1. **What sort of future did they envision for the disciples?**

   a. James, John, their mother

   b. Jesus

2. **How well did they grasp that there were things they didn't know about the future?**

   a. James, John, their mother

   b. Jesus

3. **What does it mean to be a leader?**

   a. according to James and John and their mother

   b. according to Jesus

What We Don't Know

Self-promoters like James and John are embarrassingly ignorant of the impression they make. The real question is never, "Lord, will you give us what we want?" but rather, "Lord, what needs to be done now? What would you have us do here, today?"

Jesus said to James and John's mother, "You don't know what you are asking." Their ignorance was obvious to him, but they were blind to it. Speaking of James and John, LeRoy Lawson writes this list of things they lacked:

- They don't *understand* the nature of the kingdom Jesus is establishing.

- They don't *know* the requirements of the jobs they're volunteering for.

- They don't *see* the suffering that lies ahead for Jesus and his band.

- They don't *sense* how offensive their request is to their fellows. They don't have the power to see themselves as others see them.

- They *lack* a saving sense of the ridiculous. They should be laughing at themselves.

- They *haven't learned* that meekness is more listening, less talking. It is being humble enough to believe that someone else may be right.

- [They] *don't know* what they don't know.
  —excerpted from LeRoy Lawson, *Blessed Are We*

The above statements point out that as humans, we know less about theology and the future than we think we do. We lack the necessary people skills and servant attitude and an understanding of what's involved in sacrifice.

- How does knowing that we lack the things listed above create humility?

- How does it harm our relationship with God when we think we know it all?

- In what circumstances do most of us easily become know-it-alls?

The Meek Have Already Inherited the Earth!

As far as Jesus is concerned, "the meek shall inherit the earth." They already have, you know. Of all living creatures since the earth was created, which ones are now missing? The great ones: the dinosaurs, the mammoths, the saber-toothed tigers. And which are still here, doing as they please, defying every attempt to exterminate them? The ants, the rats, the amoebas, the meekest of the animal kingdom. If you don't believe me, please give me your recipe for getting rid of roaches.

—excerpted from LeRoy Lawson, *Blessed Are We*

MORE EVIDENCE!

1.

2.

3.

4.

5.

Five

The Diet for Building Character Muscles

[T]his is how] the Pharisees went wrong. Scrupulously observing every jot and tittle of the Law, they managed to be superpious without being godly. . . . But they were the best, or at least the strictest, of their religious contemporaries.

For the Christian, [however,] the focus of righteousness is not on attaining a higher degree of spiritual attainment. . . . It isn't on self at all, because Christ has already taken care of our personal needs. He has made us one with himself.

Micah described it most simply, this righteousness that God expects of his people. You'll notice that the right thing is always in relation to other people. "He has showed you, O man, what is good. And what does the Lord require of you? To act justly and to love mercy and to walk humbly with your God" (Micah 6:8).

Acting justly, loving mercy, and walking humbly with God exhibit love for God. "To walk in his ways" is the definition of righteousness.

—LeRoy Lawson, *Blessed Are We*

Central Theme	Thirsting for righteousness doesn't mean trying to be super-pious, but behaving justly, loving mercy, and walking humbly with God.
Lesson Aim	Group members will examine a biblical example of pursuing righteousness and explore necessary elements of this righteousness.
Bible Background	Matthew 5:6; Luke 10:38-42; John 12:1-8
For Further Study	Read Chapter 5 of *Blessed Are We*.

lasses

BUILDING COMMUNITY

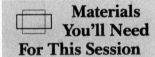

Say to class members, **Say the first thing that comes to your mind when I say the key word.** Then say the key word: *righteousness.* Try to get as many responses as possible without asking for lengthy explanations. Then if you have time, discuss reasons for their responses.

Explain, **Let's try to come up with some good news/bad news stories in which someone seems to be doing something good, but the bad news is that he's doing it for wrong reasons or in wrong ways. For example:**
   The good news is: Brad is helping out at the homeless shelter.
   The bad news is: he shows contempt for the clients.
   If class members have trouble coming up with something, offer a few good news phrases for them to respond to: Brad prays every day, or Brad loves his family, or Brad has just landed a new job.

CONSIDERING SCRIPTURE

Have the class form two groups and assign one of today's passages about Mary to each group: Luke 10:38-42 and John 12:1-8. Display Transparency 5, "Heart Examinations," and refer to the chart at the top. Explain, **Both passages have three main characters: Jesus, Mary, and someone who criticizes Mary. Read your assigned passage and discuss the questions in the middle of the transparency.**
   After a few minutes, ask groups to report their answers.

   1. What was in Mary's heart? Based on Jesus' judgment (and he knew the hearts of people according to Mark 2:8 and Luke 5:22), Mary's heart was pure and devoted to him.
   2. What seems to have been in the heart of her critics (Martha, Judas)? Jesus judged Martha's heart to be distracted and Judas's to be greedy.
   3. In what way does Mary's critic (Martha, Judas) appear to be more righteous than she? Martha appeared to be efficient and hardworking. Judas appeared to be charitable.

Word Association
5-8 minutes

OPTION
**Good News/
Bad News Story**
5-8 minutes

**Materials
You'll Need
For This Session**

Resource Sheets 5A, 5B, Transparency 5, pens or pencils, colored pens, chalk and chalkboard.

Heart Exams
10-15 minutes

If time permits, ask groups to summarize their answers. Then ask, **How did Mary demonstrate the truth of today's Beatitude, "Blessed are those who hunger and thirst for righteousness, for they will be filled" (Matthew 5:6)?** Her hunger and thirst for God seemed to be filled. Jesus said she chose the better part, and by her contentment at his feet, it seems to have been satisfying.

OPTION
Word Exploration
10-12 minutes

Distribute copies of Resource Sheet 5A, "Mary's Thirst for Righteousness," and introduce it by saying something like this: **The concept of righteousness is easily misunderstood. In both of today's passages, people criticized Mary. Righteousness can be confusing to others and it's not always what we think it is.** Throw out these questions for a few minutes: **What does righteousness really mean? Is it action? Is it an activity of the heart?**

After a few minutes of discussion, say to class members, **In the box at the bottom of the sheet, write a phrase or two that you think should be included in the definition of righteousness.** Give class members a few minutes, and then have volunteers read their phrases. If you wish, combine their phrases to write a complete definition on the chalkboard.

OPTION
Exploring Misconceptions
5-10 minutes

If the previous discussion went well, you may wish to continue it by reading the excerpt from *Blessed Are We* at the beginning of the session. Ask class members, **How did the Pharisees get righteousness wrong?**

If you wish, read Matthew 5:20, ("For I tell you that unless your righteousness surpasses that of the Pharisees and the teachers of the law, you will certainly not enter the kingdom of heaven") and ask, **How could someone be better than the Pharisees?** Use Jesus' diatribe against the righteousness of the Pharisees (Matthew 23:1-39) also, especially verse 23, in which justice, mercy, and faithfulness are mentioned.

TAKING THE NEXT STEP

Snapshots of Righteousness
10 minutes

Display Resource Sheet 5B, "What Does Righteousness Look Like?" and say to class members, **Micah 6:8 offers practical guidelines for what righteousness looks like.** Read it at the top of the handout. **Let's pretend we're photographers for a newspaper that wants to promote righteousness. We're planning to put together a page for our newspaper with photos of people behaving in righteous ways—even though they aren't thinking about it. Let's brainstorm—in what situations would we love to catch people?**

Have them form groups and write their suggestions in the appropriate column of the sheet. If their suggestion doesn't fit a category or encompasses all of them, put it in the bottom section without columns. If time permits, ask groups to share their ideas.

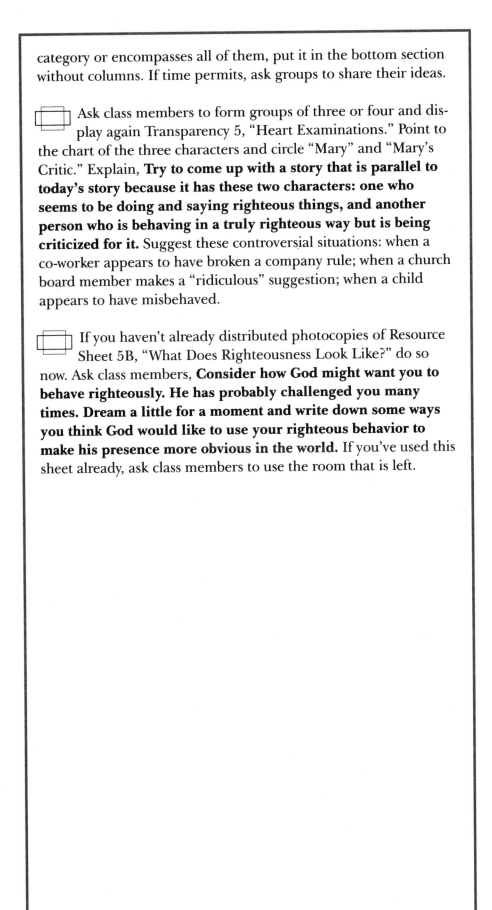

OPTION
Parallel Story
10-15 minutes

Ask class members to form groups of three or four and display again Transparency 5, "Heart Examinations." Point to the chart of the three characters and circle "Mary" and "Mary's Critic." Explain, **Try to come up with a story that is parallel to today's story because it has these two characters: one who seems to be doing and saying righteous things, and another person who is behaving in a truly righteous way but is being criticized for it.** Suggest these controversial situations: when a co-worker appears to have broken a company rule; when a church board member makes a "ridiculous" suggestion; when a child appears to have misbehaved.

OPTION
God's Dreams for Me
5-7 minutes

If you haven't already distributed photocopies of Resource Sheet 5B, "What Does Righteousness Look Like?" do so now. Ask class members, **Consider how God might want you to behave righteously. He has probably challenged you many times. Dream a little for a moment and write down some ways you think God would like to use your righteous behavior to make his presence more obvious in the world.** If you've used this sheet already, ask class members to use the room that is left.

PLAN TWO  **$\mathcal{G}$roups**

BUILDING COMMUNITY

1. Can you think of a time when you were eager to do the right thing—instead of feeling obligated to do the right thing? (It may have involved a relationship with a teacher or mentor or child.)

2. What usually makes the difference in wanting to do the right thing rather than having to? (Often it's relationships and loyalty; other times, it's seeing the benefits of doing the right thing.)

OPTION
3. Think of someone you've known who tried to do the right thing. Which category did he or she fit into?
goody two-shoes   **boring habit keeper**
quietly cooperative   **cheerfully helpful**

CONSIDERING SCRIPTURE

Read Luke 10:38-42.

1. What word in verse 39 best describes Mary? Which word in verse 40 best describes Martha? ("Listening" and "distracted" would be good choices.)

2. How do these words compare?

3. What did Jesus mean when he said, "only one thing is needed"?

4. What would you say to someone who says this proves Christians are "so heavenly minded that they're no earthly good"?

Read John 12:1-8.

5. Verse 1 says this took place "six days before the Passover," which would have been roughly two weeks before Jesus' death. How does that help us understand the passage, especially the reference to "burial" in verse 7?

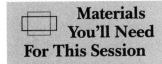

Materials You'll Need For This Session

Reproducible sheet:
Resource Sheet 5A.

OPTION
Accountability Partners
Have partners meet and talk about ways they've behaved more like Martha and Judas than Mary. Urge them to explore with each other Question 3 above about how God is calling them to deeper righteousness.

OPTION
Worship Ideas
Read Psalm 7 together as an act of worship. Song Suggestions: "Seek Ye First" by Karen Lafferty; "Righteous One" by Bruce Miller and Teresa Miller.

OPTION
Memory Verse
"Martha, Martha," the Lord answered, "you are worried and upset about many things, but only one thing is needed. Mary has chosen what is better, and it will not be taken away from her" (Luke 10:41, 42).

---

6. Contrast what seemed to be in Mary's heart with what seemed to be in Judas's heart.

7. What would be a act of devotion in today's terms comparable to Mary's (involving a year's worth of time or money)?

8. How did Martha and Judas have a skewed concept of what it meant to be righteous?

Read Matthew 5:6.

9. What would be an example of someone hungering and thirsting for righteousness?

TAKING THE NEXT STEP

1. Based on these passages of Scripture and what you've read about Mary, how would you describe righteousness? (Distribute photocopies of Resource Sheet 5A, "Mary's Thirst for Righteousness," if you wish.)

2. Quote Micah 6:8 or read the excerpt in the introduction of the session. ("He has showed you, O man, what is good. And what does the LORD require of you? To act justly and to love mercy and to walk humbly with your God.") **What categories of righteous behavior are offered in this passage?**

3. Using Micah 6:8 as a guideline for righteousness, what kinds of things is God calling you to do that involve living justly, loving mercy, or walking humbly with God?

Heart Examinations

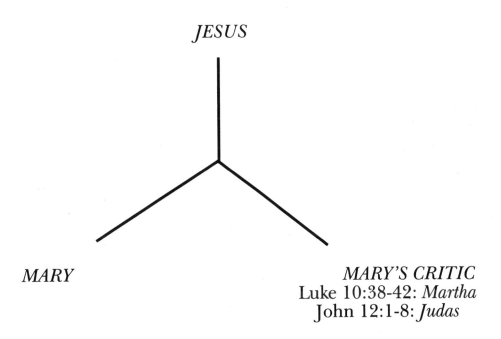

JESUS

MARY

MARY'S CRITIC
Luke 10:38-42: *Martha*
John 12:1-8: *Judas*

What was in Mary's heart?

What seems to have been in her critic's heart?

**In what way does Mary's critic (Martha, Judas)
appear to be more righteous than she?**

Mary's Thirst for Righteousness

Contrary to popular opinion, those who hunger and thirst for righteousness (not for superpiety or for the appearance of holiness, but for genuine righteousness) seem to live on a higher plane than others. We look up to them. We admit we're not up to their standard ourselves. They seem somehow to be more alive, more interesting, more in tune with themselves than the rest of us are. They are the saints of whom Frederick Buechner writes, "Only saints interest me as a writer. There is so much life in them. They are so in touch with, so transparent to, the mystery of things that you never know what to expect from them." He extols a saint as a life-giver, a human being "with the same sorts of hang-ups and abysses as the rest of us, but if a saint touches your life, you become alive in a new way."

Do these descriptions explain, at least in part, the fascination Jesus held for his friend Mary? For her, Jesus had "so much life" in him, was "so in touch with, so transparent to, the mystery of things," his touch made you "come alive in a new way;" he was so "all of a piece" he "could not be or do otherwise." Absorbing his soul-expanding words, she sat at his feet oblivious to everything else. Her sister's remonstrances couldn't move her. She was transfixed.

The kitchen beckoned Martha, and she obeyed. Mary could not be bothered by the merely *urgent;* Jesus was introducing her to the truly *important.* She wanted more. He was, from Buechner's perspective, the ultimate saint. She hungered to know Jesus better, to hear him more clearly, to be drawn into the kingdom where he was more present even than in her home. She had glimpsed eternal reality. The dishes could wait.

—excerpted from LeRoy Lawson, *Blessed Are We*

DEFINITION: *Righteousness*

What Does Righteousness Look Like?

"He has showed you, O man, what is good. And what does the LORD require of you?
To act justly and to love mercy and to walk humbly with your God" (Micah 6:8).

TO ACT JUSTLY	TO LOVE MERCY	TO WALK HUMBLY WITH YOUR GOD

Six

Heavenly Mercy!

At a Food for the Hungry seminar a couple of years ago, a man in the audience asked the presenter, a veteran of many years of famine relief work, "How do you handle compassion fatigue?" I was glad to hear the answer, because our church is bombarded with requests from people dropping in for a handout and from agencies of every kind writing for dollars to get them through their latest emergency. After a while, you turn a deaf ear. You can't bear to hear yet another plea. The seminar leader responded quietly, "You simply do what you can." Then he quoted Larry Ward, Food for the Hungry's founder. "It comes down to one life," Ward would tell his coworkers. "People die one at a time. We can help them one at a time."

—LeRoy Lawson, *Blessed Are We*

Central Theme	Merciful people respond to the needs of people they know, and know about, in simple ways without self-consciousness.
Lesson Aim	Group members will look at a biblical example of mercy and consider how simple, selfless mercy is played out in life.
Bible Background	Matthew 5:7; Luke 10:25-37
For Further Study	Read Chapter 6 of *Blessed Are We*.

Classes

BUILDING COMMUNITY

 Remind class members that the previous session dealt with hungering for righteousness and explain that this one is about mercy. Ask, **What color do you associate most with mercy? With justice?**

Write these words on the chalkboard: vengeance, justice, mercy.

Then explain to class members: **I'll tell you about a situation and I want you to give it three endings. The first ending should illustrate vengeance; the second, justice; the third, mercy.**

Read the first situation below and then ask class members to suggest possible endings in each of the three categories. If you have time, use the second situation also.

1) You walk up to a small group of people and it becomes obvious that the sentence someone is finishing is derogatory about you. (With this one, class members may suggest that ignoring it is the merciful choice. That's true, but is there a response that would be even more merciful?)

2) A neighbor child climbs over your fence and eats the cherry tomatoes off the plants you've worked hard to cultivate.

CONSIDERING SCRIPTURE

Explain that **today's theme comes from the Beatitude, "Blessed are the merciful, for they will be shown mercy" (Matthew 5:7) and that today's passage is an example of that.** Have a volunteer read Luke 10:25-37 aloud. Then distribute copies of Resource Sheet 6A, "Weapons of Mercy." Explain, **The young law expert used the weapons of his sharp mind and his tongue. What weapons did the Samaritan use to show mercy? Pick a few of them and then design a coat of arms that shows the weapons of mercy he used.** Put out colored pens in the room and suggest they block off the inside of the shield into four quadrants.

If class members are reluctant to participate because they don't like drawing, urge them to use symbols such as a dollar sign for money, a clock to represent time, an adhesive bandage

Color Association
5-8 minutes

OPTION
Finishing Stories
8-10 minutes

Materials You'll Need For This Session

Resource Sheets 6A, 6B (optional: twice as many copies of Resource Sheet 6A), Transparency 6, pens or pencils, chalk and chalkboard, colored pens.

Coat of Arms
10-15 minutes

to represent his knowledge of first aid; stick figure hands to represent physical help. Detailed drawing would take too long anyway.

After a few minutes, ask class members to show their shields to the rest of the class.

OPTION
Imagination Invasion (Jesus)
10-15 minutes

After reading Luke 10:25-37, explain to class members, **Imagine Jesus spinning this story in his mind, as the clever expert of the law questioned him. You can imagine Jesus thinking,** *Let's shock this man. Why don't I make the main character a Samaritan? Why don't I . . . ?* Ask class members to examine the story and search for other details that must have shocked the exacting law expert.

If you wish, distribute copies of Resource Sheet 6B, "Simple, Selfless Mercy," to help class members get more ideas about the details of the passage. They might notice these shocking details:
• the passing by of the religious men;
• the Samaritan helping the Jew by touching him with his hands (Samaritans would have known and understood Jewish laws of purification that prevented their touching Samaritans);
• the Samaritan cared for the Jew's future by setting him up in the inn;
• the Samaritan being generous with the Jewish innkeeper.

OPTION
Imagination Invasion (Samaritan)
8-12 minutes

Ask class members, **What might have gone through this fictional Samaritan's mind as he saw the Jew**? He may have wondered, Should I help him? Shouldn't I? Draw a vertical line down the center of the chalkboard and write "Leave" on one side and "Help" on the other. Ask them to suggest items for each side. If you have not already done so, distribute copies of Resource Sheet 6B, "Simple, Selfless Mercy," to help them consider the situation in more detail.

TAKING THE NEXT STEP

Listing
10-15 minutes

Display Transparency 6, "What the Samaritan Did Right," and point out how the Samaritan served in simple ways without self-consciousness. Read both columns of the first two examples on the chart and ask class members to suggest other simple, selfless things the Samaritan did. Write these in the left column. (Some examples: He didn't make a big deal out of it by asking for thanks or announcing himself. He was generous with the person he asked to help him, the innkeeper).

After each of their suggestions, ask them also, **How do we sometimes get it wrong?** and write that in the right column.

Ask class members, **How have you tried to solve the problem of compassion fatigue—when people feel that after giving for years they haven't made a dent and they've had enough?** If you wish, use the introductory paragraph to this lesson to get the discussion started.

Distribute additional photocopies of Resource Sheet 6A, "Weapons of Mercy," and ask class members to draw weapons of mercy they have as a personal coat of arms. Urge them to use symbols as stated above. Use pencils only to save time. As they finish, ask, **Look at the weapons of mercy you've drawn. In what current situations do you once again need them?**

OPTION
Troubling Question
10-12 minutes

OPTION
Personal Weapons of Mercy
5-7 minutes

roups

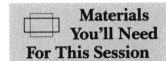 **Materials You'll Need For This Session**

Reproducible sheet: Resource Sheet 6B (optional).

BUILDING COMMUNITY

1. Tell about a time you felt mercy for someone and it surprised you—perhaps for an elderly person or a confused immigrant or a small child.

2. When have you been the recipient of mercy? On the road-side? In a committee meeting?

CONSIDERING SCRIPTURE

Read Luke 10:25-37.

1. In what way did the expert in the law "test" Jesus?

2. Does it surprise you that Jesus' quote comes from the Old Testament, showing that the Old Testament law was actually based on love? Why or why not?

3. What does the phrase "he wanted to justify himself" (v. 29) tell us about the attitude of the law expert?

4. Why do you think Jesus chose to portray the two unmerciful men as very religious men (as the expert of the law no doubt was)?

5. In what simple, concrete ways did the Samaritan help the man? (You may wish to distribute copies of Resource Sheet 6B, "Simple, Selfless Mercy" to help group members get a better picture of the Samaritan as Jesus portrayed him.)

6. What could the Samaritan have done if he had wanted attention for doing his good deed? (Probably very little. Samaritans were despised and perhaps he would have been cursed for even touching the Jew.)

7. If Jesus were inventing this story today in your culture, who would he have chosen to be the despised Samaritan? (a Middle-Eastern terrorist? a skinhead? a Ku Klux Klanner?)

OPTION
Accountability Partners
Have accountability partners meet during the week to discuss situations in mercy they may be seeing for the first time. Encourage them to look at Question 2 (Taking the Next Step), examine honestly the hardness of their heart, and pray for each other.

OPTION
Worship Ideas
Read Psalm 86 together as an act of worship. Song Suggestions: "Let the Walls Fall Down" by Bill Batstone, Anne Barbour, and John Barbour; and "Freely, Freely" by Carol Owens.

OPTION
Memory Verse
"Blessed are the merciful, for they will be shown mercy" (Matthew 5:7).

8. If Jesus were inventing this story today in your culture, who would he have chosen to be the expert in the law?

OPTION
Read Matthew 5:7

9. What does this verse have in common with a verse used in the last session: "He has showed you, O man, what is good. And what does the Lord require of you? To act justly and to love mercy and to walk humbly with your God" (Micah 6:8)?

10. In light of today's passage on the Good Samaritan, what do you think it means to "love mercy," as stated in Micah 6:8?

TAKING THE NEXT STEP

1. What kind of situations do we regularly stumble upon that call for showing mercy? At work? At home?

2. The priest and Levite seemed to have a heart bent on distancing themselves—either because of safety or time pressure. What do you believe is key to melting hard hearts?

OPTION
3. Based on this passage, we might take the charity solicitations in the mail more seriously. How do we go about that wisely?

Weapons of Mercy

Simple, Selfless Mercy

The Samaritan practiced the love Christians talk about, but fall short of practicing. We've traveled the lonely roads and seen the victims of life's brutality—and like the priest and the Levite, we've crossed over to the other side, rationalizing that we are in a hurry and it would be dangerous to stop and probably the man got what he had coming to him anyway and . . . and . . . and.

Why, when others stepped around the victim on the road to Jericho, did the Samaritan come to the rescue? Surely he, too, had pressing appointments. No doubt he could tell that the victim was a Jew—and Jews and Samaritans had no truck with each other. The racial animosity between them was deep and bitter. Don't you imagine he was as reluctant to become involved as anyone else?

So why did he do it? My guess is that his benevolence grew out of personal experience. He had been a victim himself. He'd been there, so he understood. Jesus had been warned about Samaritans all his life; they were a despised race. As an alien among foreigners, the Samaritan was no stranger to mental and perhaps even physical abuse. He may even have been rescued in the past by some merciful soul, perhaps—one would like to think—by a sympathetic Jew. His empathy moved him to action.

The careful Samaritan, gently attending ugly wounds, lifting a broken man onto his donkey, arranging for his stay in the inn, not haggling over the price of the room, taking on himself any additional expenditures—his every merciful act is a thing of beauty.

If the Samaritan's tenderness weren't so rare, there wouldn't be a story here. But mercy is beautiful in large measure because it is so uncommon.

—excerpted from LeRoy Lawson, *Blessed Are We*

What the Samaritan Did Right

(THAT MORE OF US NEED TO DO)

WHAT HE DID	HOW WE (SOMETIMES) GET IT WRONG
He did what needed to be done.	We think what we do isn't valid unless we solve the entire problem. (He didn't launch a Jerusalem-to-Jericho traveler safety program.)
The Samaritan used the resources he had.	a. He didn't worry about "wasting" what he had. b. He didn't feel the burden to do a fund-raiser for the man.

Seven

The Best Kind of Absent-Mindedness

Several years ago I read Philip Hallie's [book], *Lest Innocent Blood Be Shed*, a moving account of how a small French village became a place of refuge for Jews fleeing the murderous Nazis. As Pastor Trocme went about organizing the effort, he first convinced his presbyterial council in the winter of 1941 to establish a village residence that would be funded by the Quakers. Then he recruited his second cousin, Daniel Trocme, to take over that residence. He thought of his cousin as "an intellectual given to rather vague ideas, and often rather absentminded, but totally free of selfishness, and possessed of a conscience without gaps." He was, in other words, pure in heart. . . .

—LeRoy Lawson, *Blessed Are We*

Central Theme	Purity of heart requires that we examine our heart for the things that do not resemble God and things that keep us away from God.
Lesson Aim	Group members will examine a biblical example of someone with a divided heart, explore ways to determine when a heart is impure and divided, and examine their own hearts.
Bible Background	Matthew 5:8; Matthew 19:16-22; Mark 10:17-22
For Further Study	Read Chapter 7 of *Blessed Are We.*

 **Classes**

BUILDING COMMUNITY

Distribute copies of Resource Sheet 7A, "Always? Sometimes? Never?" and ask class members to fill them out. When they're finished, ask brave class members to volunteer their answers. Explain, **Today's session is about looking at mixed motives—which can lead to an impure heart.**

Bring three magnets. Place one on a table and then place the other two on either side. Let one outer magnet get closer to the inner one and draw it near. Then do the same with the other. Ask, **If this middle magnet were a person, how easy would it be to go anywhere? How might he or she feel inside? This is what it's like to have a divided heart.**

CONSIDERING SCRIPTURE

Read Matthew 19:16-22 together. Display Transparency 7, "Divided Heart Disease" and ask class members, **What evidence do you see of the rich young ruler's devotion to God? Use phrases from the passage itself as "evidence."** Write their ideas under "Heart for God." They might note:

- "get eternal life" (v. 16). At least he was interested in this—many people are not.
- "All these I have kept" (v. 20). He had actually obeyed all those commands.
- What do I still lack? (v. 20) He acknowledged his spiritual poverty—or perhaps he was fishing for Jesus to say he lacked nothing!
- He went away sad (v. 22). He seemed disappointed that following Christ would be so difficult.
  Ask, **What evidence do you see of his devotion to his possessions?** Write their answers under "Heart for Self."
- "He went away" (v. 22). He apparently didn't follow Christ because it would be too difficult to sell his possessions.
  Tie this in with today's Beatitude: **Consider the Beatitude, "Blessed are the pure in heart, for they will see God" (Matthew 5:8). In what way was the rich young man impure in his heart?** He wasn't purely devoted to God, but to his possessions with which he couldn't part.

Self-Quiz
5-10 minutes

OPTION
Object Lesson
3-5 minutes

Scripture Search
10-15 minutes

Materials You'll Need For This Session

Resource Sheets 7A, 7B, Transparency 7, pens or pencils, chalk and chalkboard, three magnets (optional).

After reading today's passage together, write this question on the chalkboard, "Was Jesus being picky?" Say to half of the class members, **Think of reasons why someone would say that Jesus was being picky with the young man.** They might come up with the following: The rich young ruler was righteous. He obeyed all those commands. ("According to his own account," says Lawson, "he seems to be hungering and thirsting for righteousness").

Tell the other half of the class members, **Defend Jesus. Explain why he wasn't being picky, but made sense.** The young man had integrity about some things, but not everything—not his money. He had a gap in conscience regarding his wealth.

Ask if either side wants to answer the other.

When the Scripture is read, you may wish to assign the following parts to three class members: narrator (vv. 16, 22), Jesus (vv. 17, 18, 19, 21), and the rich young ruler (vv. 16, 18, 20).

TAKING THE NEXT STEP

Distribute copies of Resource Sheet 7B, "A Conscience Without Gaps," and ask class members to form small groups. Ask a class member to read the text aloud and then pose the first question. If you wish, follow up by asking, **Instead of being devoted to God, the heart can be partly devoted to God and to what else?** (Self-promotion, acquiring of possessions, feeling good about one's self.)

Ask the second question, and after a few minutes, ask class members to tell which phrase they chose. Don't ask them to tell why they chose it unless they offer that information.

For the third question, explain, **Answer this question aloud only if you wish.**

Have the class form groups of three or four. Explain, **Let's expand on the man's question, "What do I still lack?" that forced a penetrating request out of Jesus. If you were to design a quiz that would help people examine their hearts for devotion to something other than God, how would the questions read? For example, On what do you spend discretionary money? Try to come up with three questions for a self-quiz.** Not all these questions will reveal a person's devotion to something other than God, of course, but one or two should give clues.

After a few minutes, ask the small groups to report.

Ask class members to ponder these two questions. **What is it you are devoted to that keeps you from following Jesus?** Wait a few minutes and ask, **What makes you feel you need this thing more than you need Christ?**

Groups

BUILDING COMMUNITY

1. SURVEY: In your opinion, which of these items most frequently draws the devotion of Christians away from God?
Work
Leisure
Possessions
Self-improvement (physical, psychological, and so on)
Other: _____

2. Why did you vote as you did?

OPTION
3. Why do we pursue these things instead of pursuing God and letting him give us the work leisure, possessions and self-improvement we need?

CONSIDERING SCRIPTURE

Read Matthew 19:16-22.

1. Consider these phrases in the man's opening question:
• **"what *good thing* must I do?"**
• **"what good thing must *I* do?"**
• **"get eternal life"**
What do these tell us about this man's view of religion and spirituality? (If you wish, distribute copies of Resource Sheet 7B, "A Conscience Without Gaps" and ask, Did the man seem to be extrinsically religious or intrinsically religious?)

2. How do you explain Jesus' reply, "Why do you ask me about what is good?" (He knew the man knew about goodness and had kept the commands (v. 20), or perhaps he saw the man's words as flattery (in Mark 10:17, the man called Jesus "Good Teacher").)

3. Why do you think Jesus replied with the commands regarding people instead of the commands regarding God (Such as, "Thou shalt have no other gods before me." See Exodus 20:1-17)?

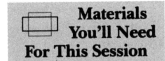
Materials You'll Need For This Session

Reproducible sheet: Resource Sheet 7B.

OPTION
Accountability Partners

Have accountability partners meet during the week and consider together Question 3: What are some things you are devoted to that keep you from following Christ? Now that they've pondered it for a few days, they may have more or different ideas. Encourage partners to accept each other's answers without judgment. That makes it easier to be honest.

OPTION
Worship Ideas

Read Psalm 51 together as an act of worship. Song Suggestions: "Change My Heart, O God" by Eddie Espinosa; "Create in Me a Clean Heart."

OPTION
Memory Verse

"Blessed are the pure in heart, for they will see God" (Matthew 5:8).

4. If the man knew he had kept all these commandments, what do you think convinced him that he still lacked something? (v. 20)

5. How did the man's sadness at being asked to give away his possessions reveal his divided heart?

6. Does it surprise you that Jesus would invite this man to follow him (with one qualification)? Why or why not?

7. What are some of the many possible reasons the man went away sad?

Read Matthew 5:8.

8. What kind of purity of heart was lacking in the rich young man?

TAKING THE NEXT STEP

1. The man's love of his possessions represents a gap in his conscience or a piece of his heart that was not devoted to God. What are some other typical things a person's heart can become devoted to? (Have someone record these items.)

2. (Pick one item from the list.) Why would people feel they need this item? What is it we fear would happen without it?

Close by asking class members to consider this question and have them answer aloud only if they wish:

3. What are some things you are devoted to that keep you from following Christ?

Always? Sometimes? Never?

Pick one of the questions below in each category
(the least embarrassing one?) and answer it.

PRAYER LIFE

- When I pray aloud, I (always, sometimes, never) try to think of something clever to say.
- When others pray aloud, I (always, sometimes, never) pay attention.
- When others pray aloud, I (always, sometimes, never) fall asleep.

LEISURE LIFE

- When I watch television, I (always, sometimes, never) ignore the people I love who interrupt me.
- When I watch television, I (always, sometimes, never) wish my life was as exciting as the main character's life in the show.
- When I watch television, I (always, sometimes, never) fall asleep.

WORK LIFE

- When I apply for a job, my first question (always, sometimes, never) is: How much will I get paid?
- When I apply for a job, my first question (always, sometimes, never) is: How much vacation will I get?
- When I apply for a job, my first question (always, sometimes, never) is: How soon will I be promoted?
- When I work, I (always, sometimes, never) fall asleep.

A Conscience Without Gaps

The pure in heart then, are of a piece, an integrated whole that runs deep. What they seem to be on the outside they are all the way to the core of their being. Hypocrisy is foreign to their nature, as Harvard psychologist Gordon Allport discovered in his study of the nature of religious behavior in relation to bigotry and prejudice. He found that a majority of adherents in religion—in any religion—could be described as *extrinsically* religious, that is, religious on the outside. They are *users* of religion. Going to church, for example, can be a relatively easy way to gain status in the eyes of the community, to win friends and make good business contacts, to become more self-confident and even more influential. So they go to church. The extrinsically religious often use their belief to defend themselves against unpleasant reality. Perhaps the most useful aspect of this "outside" religion, however, is its self-sanctioning quality. Such believers assure themselves that God sees things exactly the way they do; they are righteous as God is righteous, because God is like them. According to Allport, the extrinsically religious person *turns to God but does not turn away from self*. Like the rich young man . . . they talk about Heaven but live very much in this world. Their religion serves *them*; it gives them a sense of security, status, and self-esteem.

On the other hand, Allport found some people who were what he called *intrinsically* religious, "religious on the inside." They love their Lord with heart and soul and mind. . . . [They] had "a deeply interiorized religious faith and were totally committed to it. Their love of God was integral and all-encompassing. It was an open faith, with room for scientific and emotional facts. Intrinsic religious love was a hunger for and commitment to oneness with God and all others."

—excerpted from LeRoy Lawson, *Blessed Are We*

1. What do these phrases have to do with having a pure heart versus a divided heart?
   - Such believers assure themselves that God sees things exactly the way they do.
   - The extrinsically religious person *turns to God but does not turn away from self*.
   - Their religion serves *them*; it gives them a sense of security, status, and self-esteem.

2. Underline the phrase or two that speaks most to you.

3. What are the gaps in your conscience—areas you don't want to discuss with God or surrender to him?

Divided Heart Disease

HEART FOR GOD | **HEART FOR SELF**

Eight

The Children of God

Even though I've made multiple trips [to the Holy Land], I'm never quite prepared for the animosity—no, the undisguised hatred—separating Israelis and Palestinians.

[Yet Jesus gave everything to bring peace] and his spiritual descendants share his passion. A contemporary example is Elias Chacour, a Palestinian Christian whose family lost their Galilean homes when the new state of Israel was carved out of Palestine. Rather than ruing his people's fate, Chacour has devoted himself to the quest for peace. For that purpose he founded the Prophet Elias Technological High School and College for students of all religious and ethnic backgrounds. Being a peacemaker, he says, "means taking the side of the oppressed, underprivileged, and persecuted without becoming one-sided against the persecutor and the oppressor. If you really want to help the oppressed, since he is always at the mercy of his oppressor, *you have to care for both—convert the oppressor and uplift the oppressed.*"

—LeRoy Lawson, *Blessed Are We*

Central Theme	Peacemakers behave like God in that they want everyone to win.
Lesson Aim	Group members will examine character quality of peacemaking and explore what it means to as a peacemaker.
Bible Background	Matthew 5:9; Luke 15:11-32
For Further Study	Read Chapter 8 of *Blessed Are We.*

lasses

BUILDING COMMUNITY

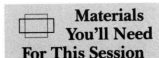

Self-Evaluation
3-5 minutes

Distribute copies of Resource Sheet 8A, "Peace, Anyone?" Read the instructions at the top of the sheet and say to class members, **Fill in the thermometers on the right and left.** (If they have trouble, encourage them to ask a friend for an opinion!)

After the above activity or in place of it, ask, **When peace is made among nations or factions or family members, what are the reasons it doesn't last?** If they don't consider these issues, bring them up: keeping peace at any price; punishing the offender unduly; settling on something that doesn't solve anything (and is therefore useless) but makes everyone equally unhappy. Don't be concerned with getting well-considered answers. These are to spark thinking and prepare for the study.

OPTION
Thought Questions
5-8 minutes

If you wish, insert one of their answers into this question: **What does God do instead of _____ (something they listed, such as making peace at any price)?**

> ### Materials You'll Need For This Session
>
> Resource Sheets 8A, 8B, Transparency 8, pens or pencils, chalk, and chalkboard.

CONSIDERING SCRIPTURE

Do & Don't List
10-15 minutes

Have the class form two or more groups and give each group a piece of paper and pencil. Say to the groups, **Read Luke 15:11-32 silently and then examine the father in the parable. Make a list of what he did and didn't do as a peacemaker. How did he bring about the growth of both sons?** Assign half the groups to: **Look at verses 11-24 and how the father handled the younger son.** Ask the other half to: **Examine verses 25-32 and note how the father handled the older son.**

As the groups are working, make two columns on the chalkboard. At the top of the first one, write: "Wrongdoers, Profligates, and Troublemakers." At the top of column 2, write: "Self-Important Defensive Know-It-Alls." After a few minutes, ask the groups to report back and record their answers.

In the first column about the younger son, they might suggest: Don't try to control this person—let him go. Don't expect him to behave in an exemplary way. Expect to watch him go through a lot of pain. Keep looking for a change of heart. Welcome and affirm a change of heart—without recounting past wrong deeds.

In column 2 about the older son, they might suggest: Expect him to be jealous of the graciousness you show to others. Don't expect him to be above lashing out at you with anger or withdrawal. Let this person express that anger. Reassure him of his value to you and others in their setting. Remind him of God's reasons to rejoice.

Don't erase the chalkboard if you plan to use this list in the case studies activity.

OPTION
Contrasting With Reality
(5-15 minutes)

After doing the above activity, examine not only the way the father behaved toward his sons, but also look at how different that is. Ask, **How would any "normal" father behave toward the rebellious, profligate son? Toward children who are arrogant and whiny?** The natural tendency is not, of course, to be peacemakers but to try to control the troublemaker and pacify (or ignore) the whiner. Note how differently this peacemaking father behaved.

TAKING THE NEXT STEP

Case Studies
10-15 minutes

Display Transparency 8, "Peacemaking in the Ordinary World of Conflict." Read the first item (ask class members to give the main character a name and write that on the transparency) and ask class members to respond to the question at the end. If you made the do and don't list above, urge class members to refer to points on the chalkboard. Do the same with each case study.

1. Affirm worker #1 when he or she is on time. Allow this employee to suffer the normal consequences of late behavior—time docked and so on. Accept worker #2's anger and affirm him or her, whenever possible. Mention to worker #2 when the first worker does something right.

2. Before the meeting, pray that you will relinquish control over this group, especially the ones who upset you. Ask God to show you their hearts and consider what would be best for their lives. You may want to write a prayer for them and take it with you to the meeting. During the meeting, expect anger from the defensive people and conflict with the ones who want change. In both groups, keep looking for a change of heart.

3. Instead of trying to convince your spouse to abandon the plan, be supportive in hearing his or her pain over being laid off and fear of starting a business. Explore the idea with your spouse by reading some books on starting small businesses or talking to people who have done this. With this supportive attitude, ask your spouse some tough questions. If you don't take a side for or against the idea, your spouse won't feel cornered into taking the other.

If class members find this activity particularly difficult, you may wish to distribute copies of Resource Sheet 8B, "Habits of Highly Effective Peacemakers" for additional ideas for help. Or, re-read some of the suggested answers in the third paragraph of the Do and Don't Activity above.

Say to class members, **Think of the last time you were involved in a conflict. Would you say you were a peacemaker, a troublemaker, somewhere in the middle, or just confused?** Let them think a minute while you distribute copies of Resource Sheet 8B, "Habits of Highly Effective Peacemakers." Then read this sheet aloud together and ask class members to tell in which of the habits listed on the sheet they wish to improve. (Also if you wish, pray for the pastors mentioned on the sheet who are still, no doubt, involved in a struggle with darkness.)

If you haven't already distributed photocopies of Resource Sheet 8B, "Habits of Highly Effective Peacemakers," do so now. Say to class members, **Circle the one or two "habits" you need most, especially with that difficult person in your life (who may be a child, a parent, a boss, a friend). If you wish, turn the sheet over and write a prayer to God about this person and your need for a spirit of peacemaking.**

Looking Back
5-8 minutes

Option
Self-Evaluation and Prayer
5-7 minutes

PLAN TWO  **Groups**

BUILDING COMMUNITY

1. How do you rate yourself as a peacemaker?
skilled   journeyman (working at it)
apprentice (starting out)   all thumbs

2. To which extreme do you tend to move?
peace at _____ making chaos
any price   wherever I go

3. In what situation have you been a peacemaker? Include situations from childhood or past jobs.

CONSIDERING SCRIPTURE

Read Luke 15:11-32.

1. **Why is the younger son's request so shocking?** (Even in our times, it would be appalling. It's the same as saying, "Let's pretend you're dead, Dad. Now, give me . . .")

2. **Why do you think the father let this younger boy go?** (You might even comment that this appears to be a "peace at any price" behavior.)

3. **List some of things the younger son probably did with the money that would have grieved and angered his father.**

4. **Do the boy's reasons for returning home seem self-centered or others-centered to you? Give a reason for your answer.**

5. **How do you think the father managed to see the boy while he was far away?** (You might wish to compare this to Jesus' miraculous ability to see from the mountainside the disciples straining at the oars of their boat when the wind was against them. See Mark 6:46-48.)

6. **What was the father's response when he saw the boy?**

7. **What did the father do when the older boy wouldn't come**

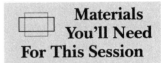

Materials You'll Need For This Session

Reproducible sheet: Resource Sheet 8B (optional).

inside to celebrate? (You may want to ask for a show of hands of those who would have let the older son stand outside until he could get his attitude straight. Going out to him showed great grace.)

8. How did the father respond to the older boy's anger and resentment?

Read Matthew 5:9.

9. In what ways was the father a peacemaker with the younger son?

10. In what ways was the father a peacemaker with the older son?

TAKING THE NEXT STEP

1. If you had been the father in the parable of the prodigal son, which son would you have had a more difficult time dealing with?

2. What is so difficult about peacemaking? (You may want to make suggestions such as setting aside resentment and personal injuries or overcoming your sense of justice with mercy. Or you may wish to distribute copies of Resource Sheet 8B, "Habits of Highly Effective Peacemakers" and let group members choose some peacemaking skills from it.)

3. In what settings is God calling you to become more of a peacemaker?

Peace, Anyone?

Use your pencil to fill in the vertical bar graphs
at the left and right to indicate
just how much of each side you are.

75%	Peace at any price!	Chaos is more fun!	75%
50%	Born to relate!	Born to be wild!	50%
25%	Never asks questions	Usually asks too many questions	25%

Habits of Highly Effective Peacemakers

"Blessed are the peacemakers" ends with a prediction: "for they will be called children of God." By whom? Is this only God's nickname for them—or will it catch on here, before they die? Why does Jesus call peacemakers children of God? Let me venture this guess: Peacemakers are children of God because they are so much like the Son of God. Like him,

- *They would rather give than take.*
Jesus said, "It is more blessed to give than to receive." They have taken him seriously, and found it so.

- *They chose to protect instead of passing by.*
Like the Good Samaritan, they can't ignore the crying need of another.

- *They share instead of stealing.*
In a world where theft is rife, peacemakers will not take what belongs to someone else; rather, they generously share the little they have with those who have less.

- *They defer instead of demanding.*
They can let others go first. They can stand while others sit. They can applaud while others take their bows.

- *They turn the other cheek.*
Peacemakers almost inevitably suffer for their faith, but the spirit of vengeance is absent. They forgive.

- *They serve the general, rather than their specific, good.*
Personal ambition, although undoubtedly a temptation, is not their dominant passion. They are eager to build the kingdom of God on earth.

- *They defend others.*
But not themselves. They are too busy to worry about their own feelings.

- *They laugh at themselves but not at others.*
Wars are waged by people who take themselves too seriously, and others not seriously enough.

- *They refuse to let others tell them what they should think about someone else.*
They think—and love—for themselves. As a result, guided by the Holy Spirit, they learn to love without prejudice. They are on everyone's side. They want everyone to win. Thus they bring peace.

—excerpted from LeRoy Lawson, *Blessed Are We*

Peacemaking in the Ordinary World of Conflict

1. You supervise a crew of people.

Worker #1 (give him or her a name) takes breaks that are too long, arrives late and then wants extra compensatory days. Worker #2 (give him or her a name as well) gets there on time and stares you down when the rebel comes in late. You feel like firing the first one and transferring the second one to another department. What do you do to be a peacemaker?

2. Some church board meetings have brought out the worst in you.

You tend to think you're right—yet it's the other people there who think they're right that upset you the most. They upset you even more than the people who want to change everything all the time! Let's say you see a meeting coming up on the calendar and you've decided to be a peacemaker. What can you do to prepare yourself? What can you do during the meeting? Afterward?

3. Things are tense between you and your spouse.

He or she has been laid off and wants to start a business—with the family savings. Your first response is absolutely not. If you were to be a peacemaker, what would be your second and third responses?

Nine

Rejected for the Right Reasons

The letter to the editor in *Time* magazine a few years ago says it all. The writer waxed indignant about the recorded "Please hold" messages you get on the phone when you're waiting for your call to be transferred to another party. To keep you dangling, the voice periodically breaks into the music to assure that your call is important and your party will be with you any moment now. Probably everybody finds these recordings irritating. For the correspondent, however, "irritating" is too soft a word for what she feels while holding. "This suffering takes endurance if not restraint," she complains.

Suffering. Endurance. Restraint. What words would she use to describe a real problem? Her exaggerated reaction illustrates the resistance Jesus' eighth Beatitude faces in an age like ours. We affluent Westerners can endure anything but discomfort. . . . In many nations, to admit to being a Christian is to invite persecution, even death. Believers in these closed nations . . . are imitating Jesus, who lived with crescendoing criticism from the beginning of his public ministry until its explosion in full-scale persecution and death.

—LeRoy Lawson, *Blessed Are We*

Central Theme	Persecution is part of the "normal" Christian life.
Lesson Aim	Group members will look at an example from the Bible of suffering to advance the gospel, and will explore ways they can support those who suffer.
Bible Background	Matthew 5:10; Acts 6:16-40
For Further Study	Read Chapter 9 of *Blessed Are We*.

Classes

BUILDING COMMUNITY

Say something like this to class members: **Let's say you are stuck on a desert island with your foot caught in a trench. You have shelter and enough food, and you know that help is coming in one year. What five things would you want most to have at your side to keep you busy? Tell the person next to you what those five things would be.**

Say to class members, **At some time you may have heard about the apostle Paul and how he was imprisoned for the gospel. Pretend—make this fun—you could grant Paul five favorite items to have next to him in prison. Based on what you already know about what he did in prison, pick those five things. Would he have wanted a few gospel tracts, for instance?**

If you have class members who are unfamiliar with the Bible, make sure they match up with a class member who is and who can fill them in on one or two things they remember about Paul being in prison. Otherwise, jog their memories with a few questions such as, **What did Paul do there? For example, what did he do that resulted in the New Testament being written? Or, Recall the story of the time he was in prison with Silas and there was an earthquake and the jailer started to kill himself.**

CONSIDERING SCRIPTURE

Write the question on the chalkboard: How could Paul have reacted to being in prison? Ask a volunteer to be ready to read Acts 16:16-40 and then offer these instructions: **As the passage is read, listen for clues that could answer the question written on the board. Paul could have complained about being a Roman citizen beaten publicly without a trial.**

Here are some ideas class members might come up with: blaming the slave girl (vv. 16-18); blaming the owners of the slave girl (vv. 19-21); focusing on how badly they were flogged (v. 23); taunting the guard (v. 23); complaining about their feet being in stocks (v. 24).

Then ask, **What did Paul do in prison?** They prayed and sang (v. 25).

Neighbor Nudge
3-5 minutes

OPTION
Paul's Neighbor Nudge Items
3-5 minutes

Materials You'll Need For This Session

Resource Sheet 9A, Transparency 9, pens or pencils, chalk and chalkboard.

Listening Teams
10-15 minutes

Have someone read Matthew 5:10 and ask, **In what way had Paul and Silas discovered the kingdom of Heaven already?** With their singing and praying, they already behaved in ways that will be common in Heaven.

Pass out pencils and pieces of paper to class members and explain, **Instead of my asking you questions, today I want you to ask each other questions.** Have the class members count off by threes. Assign the passages this way:

Number	Write a question from this passage:
1	Acts 16:16-22
2	Acts 16:23-34
3	Acts 16:35-40

When they're finished, collect all the #1 questions and ask a volunteer to read Acts 16:16-22 aloud. Ask the #1 questions. Do the same with the other two sets of questions.

TAKING THE NEXT STEP

Introduce the activities below by distributing copies of Resource Sheet 9A, "Persecuted for Righteousness' Sake," and have class members take turns reading each bulleted item. Read the summary statements yourself.

Display Transparency 9, "What Is Our Role?" and have the class form groups of five or six. Ask class members to consider the questions on the transparency and write answers. Urge them to consider the Scriptures in the box as they answer their questions.

- *What needs to happen in our hearts?* We need to allow our hearts to be broken by the pain of our fellow Christians who suffer.
- *What needs to change about our understanding of the world?* The typical Christian is not a typical American. Most of the world struggles much more economically, and Christians are martyred.
- *What needs to change about our understanding of the Christian faith?* We need to accept that suffering is "normal."
- *What do we need to do?* We need to pray for God's kingdom to advance, and for strength for struggling Christians. We can support missionaries and believers overseas in both prayer and finances.

As class members work with the questions on Transparency 9, "What Is Our Role?", they might want to consider the following statements from the opposing point of view. Write one or more on the chalkboard and ask small groups to consider them.

OPTION
Question Box
10-15 minutes

Introduction
3-5 minutes

OPTION
Small Group Discussion
10-15 minutes

OPTION
Opposing Ideas
10-15 minutes

102 • Classes • Session Nine

- Who cares about Christians overseas?
- There's nothing we can do to help Christians overseas anyway.
- It's hopeless to try to help Christians overseas because their corrupt governments are in charge.
- If I help, I'll be interfering with their martyrdom, which is God's will, right?

Instead of writing the above statements on the chalkboard, play them out in the front of the class. Cross your arms in front of you, and state these ideas as if you believe them. This approach may help those who think this way to feel less like the "bad guys" and therefore listen more attentively. Also, the impact of the discussion might be more dramatic and memorable for class members.

Option
Opposing Ideas
Role Play
10-15 minutes

Groups

BUILDING COMMUNITY

1. What kinds of circumstances make it easy for you to feel persecuted?

2. When, if at all, have you been persecuted for "righteousness' sake" and it had nothing to do with your own shortcomings?

3. Can you think of anyone else who has been persecuted for "righteousness' sake"?

CONSIDERING SCRIPTURE

Read Acts 16:16-40.

1. How did the slave girl know about Paul and Christianity?

2. Compare the true motives of the slave girl's owners with the cause they espoused.

3. What tortures were Paul and Silas put through?

4. How did Paul and Silas spend their time in prison?

5. How did Paul and Silas respond to their opportunity to escape?

6. The jailer asked, What must I do to be saved?" How would he have known to ask that such a question of his prisoners? (From hearing the content of the singing and praying, from hearing Paul and Silas preach around Philippi before they were arrested.)

7. Contrast the jailer's first interaction with Paul and Silas (vv. 23, 24) and his last (v. 34).

8. In what ways did the jailer minister to Paul and Silas?

9. No reason is explicitly stated for Paul and Silas's release.

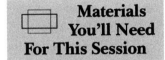

Materials You'll Need For This Session

Reproducible sheets: Resource Sheets 9A, 9B, also photocopies of Transparency 9.

OPTION
Accountability Partners
Have accountability partners meet and, if you wish, give them photocopies of Transparency 9, "What Is Our Role?" to discuss. Urge them to pray that God would change their hearts. Explain that accountability partners are especially helpful in this area because it isn't pleasant and we might prefer to ignore it. As partners, we remind each other by telling about how God is speaking to us in this area.

OPTION
Worship Ideas
Read Psalm 22 together as an act of worship. Song Suggestions: "I Will Follow" by John Barbour and Anne Barbour; "I Have Decided to Follow Jesus" (source unknown).

OPTION
Memory Verse
"Blessed are those who are persecuted because of righteousness, for theirs is the kingdom of heaven" (Matthew 5:10).

What else in the narrative might have convinced the magistrates to release Paul and Silas? (the earthquake, the testimony of the jailer)

Read also Matthew 5:10.

10. Picture for a moment the irony of Paul and Silas with their badly beaten bodies (Acts 16:23) encouraging the Christians at Lydia's home (Acts 16:40). How did Paul and Silas exemplify this Beatitude?

TAKING THE NEXT STEP

Distribute photocopies of Resource Sheet 9A, "Persecuted for Righteousness' Sake" and have group members read it silently.

1. What can we do to focus on those who suffer for Christ instead of making a big deal out of our small discomforts? If you wish, read the introductory excerpt.

2. Distribute copies of Resource Sheet 9B, "Praying for Those Who Are Persecuted for Righteousness' Sake." Ask, **What on this sheet is most shocking to you?**

3. Option: Read Resource Sheet 9B, "Praying for Those Who Are Persecuted for Righteousness' Sake" together as a group prayer. Prepare by asking several volunteers to read the italicized statements. Ask the rest of the group to read the phrases that are designated "All." Explain, **After each italicized phrase is read, all will respond with the phrase that follows it.** Close in prayer for the Christian martyrs across the world.

Persecuted for Righteousness' Sake

Jesus' disciples have faced hardship of every kind.
Christian history has been written, we are often reminded,
in the blood of martyrs.

Cuba: Pastor Orson Vila was imprisoned for conducting "illicit" religious meetings; he remains under house arrest.

Algeria: Islamic fundamentalist terrorists slit the throats of seven French Trappist monks.

Sudan: Five Nubian Christian women were sentenced to death for apostasy. Ten people were arrested for converting to Christianity.

Pakistan: At least five Christians died while in police custody. A blasphemy law mandates the death penalty for anyone convicted of blaspheming against the Prophet Muhammad.

Saudi Arabia: Seven Indian nationals were arrested for conducting private Christmas services. Conversion from Islam to any other religion is a crime punishable by death.

Laos: Northern provincial officials began a campaign to close down churches. Christians have been forced to sign affidavits renouncing faith and promising to stop all Christian activities.

Vietnam: Dozens of church leaders were imprisoned for their religious activities.

North Korea: Religious literature cannot be imported. Missionaries are denied entry, and only three Christian congregations are licensed for 25 million people.

SUMMARY:
- an estimated 250,000 Christians are martyred annually
- the average Christian today lives [not in the U.S., but] in a developing country, speaks a non-European language, and exists under the threat of murder, imprisonment, torture and rape.

—adapted from LeRoy Lawson, *Blessed Are We*

Praying for Those Who Are Persecuted for Righteousness' Sake

Cuba: Pastor Orson Vila was imprisoned for conducting "illicit" religious meetings; he remains under house arrest.

ALL: Blessed are those who are persecuted because of righteousness, for theirs is the kingdom of heaven.

Sudan: Five Nubian Christian women were sentenced to death for apostasy. Ten people were arrested for converting to Christianity.

ALL: Dear friends, do not be surprised at the painful trial you are suffering, as though something strange were happening to you.

Pakistan: At least five Christians died while in police custody. A blasphemy law mandates the death penalty for anyone convicted of blaspheming against the Prophet Muhammad.

ALL: But rejoice that you participate in the sufferings of Christ, so that you may be overjoyed when his glory is revealed.

Laos: Northern provincial officials began a campaign to close down churches. Christians have been forced to sign affidavits renouncing faith and promising to stop all Christian activities.

ALL: If you are insulted because of the name of Christ, you are blessed, for the Spirit of glory and of God rests on you.

North Korea: Religious literature cannot be imported. Missionaries are denied entry, and only three Christian congregations are licensed for 25 million people.

ALL: Blessed are those who are persecuted because of righteousness, for theirs is the kingdom of heaven.

— facts excerpted from LeRoy Lawson, *Blessed Are We*
Scripture: Matthew 5:10; 1 Peter 4:12-14

What Is Our Role?

What needs to happen in our hearts?

What needs to change about our understanding of the world?

What needs to change about our understanding of the
Christian faith?

What do we need to do?

HELP!

- If one part suffers, every part suffers with it; if one part is honored, every part rejoices with it (1 Corinthians 12:26).

- Do nothing out of selfish ambition or vain conceit, but in humility consider others better than yourselves. Each of you should look not only to your own interests, but also to the interests of others (Philippians 2:3, 4).

- Therefore go and make disciples of all nations, baptizing them in the name of the Father and of the Son and of the Holy Spirit, and teaching them to obey everything I have commanded you. And surely I am with you always, to the very end of the age (Matthew 28:19, 20).

- Dear friends, do not be surprised at the painful trial you are suffering, as though something strange were happening to you. But rejoice that you participate in the sufferings of Christ, so that you may be overjoyed when his glory is revealed. If you are insulted because of the name of Christ, you are blessed, for the Spirit of glory and of God rests on you (1 Peter 4:12-14).

Ten

On Getting What's Coming to You

P utting the three stories [from Matthew 25—the ten virgins, the talents, the sheep and the goats] together, we are to understand that Jesus desires disciples who are aware that the Lord could return at any time (vv. 1-13), who are good stewards of the resources God has provided (vv. 14-30), and who look for opportunities to help others in need (vv. 31-46). They do good deeds that in and of themselves seem less religious than humane; they are acts of kindness that should be routine among human beings.

What a different concept of religion this is. The Lord has nothing to say in this chapter about preparing for Judgment Day through burnt sacrifices or the observance of holy days or holding the proper doctrines.

—LeRoy Lawson, *Blessed Are We*

Central Theme   Believers can prepare for Jesus' return with compassionate, pro-active, selfless service.

Lesson Aim   Group members will examine the pro-active, selfless behavior of the "sheep" and discover what such behavior would look like in their everyday lives.

Bible Background   Matthew 25:31-46

For Further Study   Read Chapter 10 of *Blessed Are We*.

Classes

BUILDING COMMUNITY

Give a chenille wire (pipe cleaner) or a "twistie" (the papered wires used in grocery stores to tie up bags of produce) and say to class members, **Bend your wire in some shape or form that somehow represents the idea of compassion to you. Don't worry about being creative or clever—just do the first thing that pops in your head.**

After a few minutes, ask class members to show their sculptures to the rest of the class and explain it. If you have more than ten class members, have them do this in groups of ten.

Ask class members, **What fictional characters from a book, comic strip, or television show demonstrate compassion? This person may have a "tough guy" image, so the compassion isn't easy for others to see.** Give them a few minutes to think, and then ask for their suggestions.

CONSIDERING SCRIPTURE

Distribute photocopies of Resource Sheet 10A,"What's the Difference?" and ask three class members to read aloud one section of today's passage: vv. 31-33, 34-40, and 41-46. Divide the class in half and say to one half, **Read verses 34-40 and answer the questions in the left column.** Say to the other half, **Read verses 41-46 and answer the questions in the right column.**

After a few minutes, ask class members from the first group to respond, then the second. Here are some ideas to add if necessary:

"Sheep" (vv. 34-40): In their outward behavior, they were proactive and helped needy people. In their hearts, they seemed to be the kind of people who felt compassionate for people in need without overlooking or ignoring them. They did not outwardly gloat, and they must not have even made a big deal of it in their hearts, because they couldn't remember their good deeds at Judgment Day.

"Goats" (vv. 41-46): They did nothing in their outward behavior to help. It could be that they thought about it and may have even debated helping or talked about it with someone else. It

Wire Sculpture
5-10 minutes

OPTION
Media Examples
(5-8 minutes)

Comparison Chart
10-15 minutes

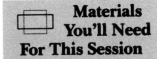

Materials You'll Need For This Session

Resource Sheets 10A, 10B, pens or pencils, chalk and chalkboard, chenille wires or "twisties."

seems that their hearts easily forgot what they saw.

Ask this question of the entire class: **In what ways are the "sheep" ready for Christ's return while the "goats" are not?** The "sheep" have shown that they have "eyes" for Jesus and for his causes in this world, even if they weren't fully conscious of it. They have behaved as Jesus did in this world and taken his love for this world seriously.

OPTION
A Letter to the Nations
10-15 minutes

After the Scripture is read, note that in this passage, Jesus specifically addressed "the nations." Write on the chalkboard: "Dear Presidents of the World," and say to class members, **Let's imagine we've been asked to write a letter to the national leaders in the world. What suggestions do we have about how nations should behave based on today's Scripture passage? Be sure to address the reasons nations don't want to help each other such as competition and world dominance.**

The "letter" should include items mentioned in the passage: feeding the hungry, giving water to the thirsty, welcoming strangers, clothing the needy, tending the sick, and forming relationships with prisoners. (List these on the chalkboard if you plan to use "Thought Question" below.)

TAKING THE NEXT STEP

Writing Prayers
10-15 minutes

Distribute copies of Resource Sheet 10B, "What Does Benevolence Look Like?" Have a volunteer read each section aloud. Then ask class members to choose one of the qualities: lack of self-consciousness, pro-activity, or the ability to see the "little ones." Say, **Ponder for a moment what it takes to selfless or to be proactive or to be willing to see the "little ones." After you've done that, turn your sheet over and write a prayer asking God to instill in you the qualities you need to be that way.**

OPTION
Listing
5-10 minutes

Prepare for the "Writing Prayers" activity by identifying qualities needed for each of the character traits listed on Resource Sheet 10B, "What Does Benevolence Look Like?" Focus on the positive qualities needed, not the negative qualities of the "goats." For example, for "Blessed are the unself-conscious" you may cite humility, having a realistic (not overblown) assessment of the effects of any good deeds you do, and not taking your own goodness too seriously. For "Blessed are the pro-active" you might list willing to risk, willing to give up time for someone else, and having initiative. And for "Blessed are those who can see the little people," basing someone's worth on God's love for them instead of their socio-economic status or what they look like or where they work, and having a welcoming heart to people you don't know and a willingness to "see" them.

If you used the above activity, "A Letter to the Nations," review the answers class members have come up with and ask, **How can we as citizens promote this—individually and as a nation?** Give them a few minutes to think about this. They might come up with support of missionaries and relief organizations, trying to put God's compassion into immigration programs, or trying to develop a fair, efficient welfare system.

OPTION
Thought Question
5-10 minutes

PLAN TWO **roups**

BUILDING COMMUNITY

1. Why do people avoid helping the needy—and sometimes avoid even talking to them?

2. When has it been easy for you to help someone in need?

3. Consider someone you've helped recently. Would it have made a difference if you had viewed your service to that person as service to Jesus himself? If so, what?

CONSIDERING SCRIPTURE

Read Matthew 25:31-33.

1. Based on these introductory verses, do you think this passage is a parable? Why or why not? (Jesus didn't say it was a parable, so it may not be. It is, however, grouped with two other parables—the parable of the ten virgins and the parable of the talents.)

2. To whom (or to what groups of people) was Jesus talking in this scene?

Read Matthew 25:34-40.

3. What does the beatitude contained in verse 34 say about who is blessed?

4. In what ways did these people encounter Jesus without knowing it?

5. Why do you think these people couldn't even remember serving Christ?

Read Matthew 25:41-46.

6. What penalty did Jesus portray for the nations on the left?

7. Neither group could remember ever seeing Jesus—so what

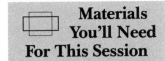
Materials You'll Need For This Session

Reproducible sheets:
Resource Sheet 10B,
Transparency 10.

Accountability Partners

Have accountability groups meet and talk about ways they can encourage each other to serve the needy and lonely. Perhaps they could do something together—Jesus advocating serving two by two (Mark 6:7-13) because it helps to have someone else along.

OPTION
Worship Ideas

Read Psalm 72 together as an act of worship. Song Suggestions: "If My People" by Eddie Smith; "Turn Your Eyes Upon Jesus" by Helen Lemmel.

OPTION
Memory Verse

"Then the King will say to those on his right, 'Come, you who are blessed by my Father; take your inheritance, the kingdom prepared for you since the creation of the world'" (Matthew 25:34).

was the difference that made the first group help, but not the second?

8. In this scene, Jesus used the way people treat the needy as a litmus test for being "righteous." What does a person's attitude toward the needy say about his or her overall heart and character?

Reread Matthew 25:34

9. In what way is this verse a beatitude?

Taking the Next Step

Display Transparency 10, "Hands and Feet of Christ."

1. If the church is to function as Jesus' body here on earth, what does the church need to do? (List answers in the right column.)

2. Since Jesus specifically addressed "nations," what does this say about how nations should behave?

Distribute photocopies of Resource Sheet 10B, "What Does Benevolence Look Like?"

3. Which character quality—being selfless, being pro-active (taking initiative), or seeing the needs of people around you— would require the most effort for you to attain? Why?

What's the Difference?

What was different about the "sheep" and the "goats"?
How did they behave differently?
What different things were going on in their hearts?

	THE "SHEEP" vv. 34-40	THE "GOATS" vv. 41-46
As they saw the hungry, thirsty person or the stranger or the naked person	Outward behavior? Likely activity of the heart?	Outward behavior? Likely activity of the heart?
After they saw the hungry, thirsty person or the stranger or the naked person	Outward behavior? Likely activity of the heart?	Outward behavior? Likely activity of the heart?

What Does Benevolence Look Like?

Blessed are the unself-conscious.

What *are* we going to look like in Heaven? . . . Whatever form our body takes, for certain there won't be any mirrors in our heavenly house. We won't need them. Primping will be out of fashion there, as will parading our religiosity to impress people (Matthew 6:1-18). . . . We won't be self-conscious in Heaven, and it's really inappropriate on earth. As those on the Master's right demonstrate, genuine compassion displays such ease in giving and grace in tending the needy that it can't even remember doing it.

Blessed are the pro-active.

Look at the verbs: You *fed* me, *gave* me drink, *invited* me in, *clothed* me, *looked* after me, *visited* me. You saw my plight and acted. You didn't wait to be asked. The initiative was yours. You weren't trying to be "religious." You weren't even thinking about God at the time; you certainly weren't trying to score points with him. You just reached out as one human being to another. Ironically, when you were *feeling* least religious, God was quite aware of what you were doing.

Blessed are those who can see the little people.

Jesus is as concerned about the "least of these brothers of mine" as he is about the greatest. No one is to be ignored.

Dr. Paul Brand has inspired countless admirers with his mission work among lepers, who are the easiest of all to overlook. For centuries they have the "least." One of Dr. Brand's patients, Sadan, once told him, "I am happy that I had the disease leprosy, Dr. Brand." The good physician looked incredulous. Sadan explained, "Without leprosy I would have spent all my energy trying to rise in society. Because of it, I have learned to care about the little people. . . ."

[These "little people" include] the children, the handicapped, the oddballs, the aging, the victimized. [The "blessed ones"] will not allow us to be satisfied that we've done enough to tear down the barriers that prevent the blind, the deaf, the abused, the mentally and emotionally disadvantaged from finding their way into and feeling at home among God's people. [These "blessed ones"] won't let us gossip about, or, what's worse, ignore the alcoholic, the drug-addicted, the victims of vicious diseases and equally vicious human predators. They wonder what more can be done for the aging, the lonely, the fatherless. Is there anyone their restless eyes don't see?

—excerpted from LeRoy Lawson, *Blessed Are We*

Hands and Feet of Christ

What did Jesus do when he was physically present here on earth?

What does the church do to manifest Jesus' presence here on earth?

- healed the sick

- raised the dead

- returned the demon-possessed to wholeness

- cared for the broken-hearted

- reached out to the prostitutes and criminals

- presented God's truth to the nations

Eleven

Of Giving and Blessing

Nothing dampens your worship quite like a calculating spirit. Wayne Watts says that while he was writing his little book, *The Gift of Giving*, God convicted him to begin giving every time he went to church. Up to then he had been giving the church a monthly check, based on his annual income. So he began to offer something whenever he attended worship, writing a check so he could keep a record of it. If he didn't have a check handy, he gave cash. He tried to keep a tally of the cash, but then, he said, God convicted him again: "You do not need to keep up with the amount of cash. Give to me simply out of a heart of love, and see how much you enjoy the service." He did—and his joy increased.

—LeRoy Lawson, *Blessed Are We*

Central Theme	Giving is accompanied not by painful sacrifice, but by joy.
Lesson Aim	Group members will look at the positive aspects of giving and explore ideas for personal giving.
Bible Background	John 13:17; Acts 20:35; 2 Corinthians 8:1-9
For Further Study	Read Chapter 11 of *Blessed Are We*.

Classes

BUILDING COMMUNITY

Write these four items on the chalkboard (or pick a few other items that might make the discussion more interesting):

- your bed
- one full day of your time
- a shirt you own that you really like
- a $50 dollar bill

Say to class members, **Choose which of these items would be the most painful to give away to someone who needed it.** Call out the first item ("your bed") and ask for a show of hands. Do the same with the other items. Then ask, **Which item would be the least painful to give away?** Ask for a show of hands for each item and ask, **Why would the item you picked be so easy to give away?**

Ask a few outgoing class members to do the following: **Think of one thing you would most dislike to give away. Don't say out loud what it is. In a few minutes, I'll ask you to describe only its shape and color.** Have class members present their item one at a time with other class members guessing. If, as the game progresses, no one guesses a particular item correctly, allow the class member to add clues such as how often the item is used or when they first got it.

If you wish, ask this question with either of the above activities: **Which is more difficult to give away, money or time? Why?**

CONSIDERING SCRIPTURE

Distribute photocopies of Resource Sheet 11A, "Word Search," and set out a variety of colored pens. Then read the instructions together and focus on the first one. Explain to class members: **Choose a colored pen and mark the positive words in the text with that pen. After you do so, put a slash from that pen in the top blank to help you remember the color you chose.** Then suggest they do the same with the other two categories (instructions 2 and 3). Finally, ask them to under-

Ranking
10-15 minutes

Materials You'll Need For This Session

Resource Sheets 11A—11C, Transparency 11, pens or pencils, chalk and chalkboard, colored pens.

OPTION
Guessing Game
5-10 minutes

OPTION
Survey
3-5 minutes

Color Coding Themes
10-15 minutes

line words related to giving. Your class members might come up with results similar to the following:

Positive words: more blessed (Acts 20:35); blessed (John 13:17); grace (2 Corinthians 8:1); welled up in extreme generosity (2 Corinthians 8:2); privilege (v. 4); sharing (v. 4); "gave themselves first to the Lord" (v. 5).

Words of joy: overflowing joy (v. 2)

Words of excitement and enthusiasm: "beyond their ability" (v. 3); pleaded (v. 4); "they did not do as we expected" (v. 5) "bring to completion this act of grace" (v. 6); excel in everything, excel in this grace of giving (v. 7); earnestness of others (v. 8).

Words about giving: rich, "through his poverty he might become rich" (v. 9).

Ask class members to volunteer their answers for each category.

Then ask, **What do you think is the theme of the 2 Corinthians passage?** That giving should be done with joy and excitement. Ask, **What does this theme tell us about giving?** It doesn't have to be painful and difficult.

OPTION
Symbol Coding
(10-15 minutes)

Mark the text as described above, but ask class members to use symbols instead of colors. For example, they could underline positive words, put brackets around words of joy, circle words of excitement or enthusiasm, and put a rectangle around words of giving. You can use Resource Sheet 11A, but ask class members to put the appropriate symbols in the blank spaces.

OPTION
Background Analysis
5 minutes

Reading 2 Corinthians 2:1-9 can raise a lot of questions if you don't know what has happened among Paul and the early churches. Display Transparency 11, "Exploring the Text," to help class members understand some of the basic facts about what had already occurred. You may wish to read the questions and have different class members read the answers.

TAKING THE NEXT STEP

Analyzing Examples
10 minutes

Distribute copies of Resource Sheet 11B, "Vignettes of Giving." Say, **As this is read, listen for signs of joy in the people who give.** Have a class member read the selections from the sheet.

Ask, **What signs of joy did you notice?** Miss McCarty quoted today's memory verse and affirmed that it's more blessed to give than receive. The Nepalese sang as they gave a second time.

OPTION
Plotting to Give
10-15 minutes

Distribute copies of Resource Sheet 11C, "Good Deeds in Secret." Read the top portion together and ask class members to complete the items on the page. Then say, **Pair up with**

someone (not anyone mentioned on your list!) and tell them some of your ideas. After the pairs have had a chance to talk, ask if they would tell the entire group some of the ideas they came up with, omitting names of those whom they'd like to help.

Put class members in groups of four and say, **Look at who is on your right. If you don't know that person, introduce yourself. Then look through your pockets, coat, or wallet and find something you can give that person—for keeps. For example, you might carry a pen or little poem or brochure you can part with.**

Give class members a few minutes to search. At first they may be astounded that you are asking them to actually give away the item. Repeat, if necessary, that this is for keeps. Give them a minute or two to get used to the idea and participate. After you're finished, ask them, **How did it feel to actually give something away on the spur of the moment?** Listen to see if anyone gave away anything of value to them.

OPTION
Giving Game
10-15 minutes

PLAN TWO roups

BUILDING COMMUNITY

Ask group members to choose a partner in the room—someone they know better than anyone else.

Materials You'll Need For This Session

Reproducible sheet: Transparency 11.

1. What kind of giver is your partner?
all-occasion gift giver   holiday giver only
once-in-a-blue moon giver   born without gift-giving gene

2. Did your partner identify you correctly? If not, which answer is more appropriate? (Just for fun, you might want to bring a pillow that partners can use to "bong" each other with if they're wrong. If you do this, hold it up before the questions, so they can enjoy teasing each other.)

OPTION
3. When have you given to a cause and received great joy from it? Urge them to consider situations that don't involve holidays—just everyday moments.

After each person answers #3, ask the rest of the group:

4. What expressions of joy did you hear from this person? (This can be words or actions or facial expressions.)

CONSIDERING SCRIPTURE

Read Acts 20:35.

1. What extra joy is found in giving instead of receiving?

Read John 13:17. (Explain that Jesus said these words after he had washed the disciples' feet.)

2. What kinds of joy do you think Jesus may have experienced as he washed the disciples' feet?

Read 2 Corinthians 8:1-9.

3. Verse 2 reminds us of how people experiencing natural

OPTION

Accountability Partners
Have partners meet and talk with each other about how God has been speaking with them since the group session about what kind of giver they would like to be.

OPTION

Worship Ideas
Read Psalm 37 together as an act of worship. Song Suggestions: "Make Me a Servant" by Kelly Willard; "Give of Your Best to the Master" by Howard B. Grose and Charlotte A. Barnard.

OPTION

Memory Verse
In everything I did, I showed you that by this kind of hard work we must help the weak, remembering the words the Lord Jesus himself said: "It is more blessed to give than to receive" (Acts 20:35).

disasters often band together and share. Have you ever experienced that kind of thing?

4. What inspires the kind of giving ("beyond their ability") described in vv. 3, 4?

5. What does it appear that Paul expected the Macedonian churches to do? (v. 5) Display Transparency 11, "Exploring the Text," to help answer this question.

6. How could Titus "bring to completion this act of grace"?

7. Describe the Corinthians as Paul described them.

8. What methods of persuasion did Paul use to urge the Corinthians to give? (He didn't command them, but he gave them the Macedonians as a positive role model to which they could compare themselves.)

9. In what ways was Christ rich? In what ways did he become poor?

TAKING THE NEXT STEP

1. When have you had a positive giving experience?

2. How would you rate your general desire to give to others?
It comes easily.   Sometimes it comes easily.
This is a struggle for me.   I'm learning more about this.

3. How easily do you associate feelings of joy with giving away something you hold dear—money, time, possessions?
Easily   Somewhat easily   Not easily at all

4. Which of these truths would help you feel more joy in giving?
A better understanding that . . .
. . . God is the true owner of my possessions, money and time.
. . . God gives me things with the intention that I give them away—to help others, to show love to them, to show them the love of Christ.
. . . when we don't want to give, we can ask God to give through us.

Word Search

1. Look through these passages of Scripture for **positive** words.
Mark them _____.

2. Look through these passages for **words relating to joy**.
Mark them _____.

3. Look through these passages for words of **excitement and enthusiasm.**
Mark them _____.

4. Look through these passages for words relating to **giving.**
Mark them _____.

In everything I did, I showed you that by this kind of hard work we must help the weak, remembering the words the Lord Jesus himself said: "It is more blessed to give than to receive" (Acts 20:35).

Now that you know these things, you will be blessed if you do them (John 13:17).

And now, brothers, we want you to know about the grace that God has given the Macedonian churches. (2) Out of the most severe trial, their overflowing joy and their extreme poverty welled up in rich generosity. (3) For I testify that they gave as much as they were able, and even beyond their ability. Entirely on their own, (4) they urgently pleaded with us for the privilege of sharing in this service to the saints. (5) And they did not do as we expected, but they gave themselves first to the Lord and then to us in keeping with God's will. (6) So we urged Titus, since he had earlier made a beginning, to bring also to completion this act of grace on your part. (7) But just as you excel in everything—in faith, in speech, in knowledge, in complete earnestness and in your love for us—see that you also excel in this grace of giving. (8) I am not commanding you, but I want to test the sincerity of your love by comparing it with the earnestness of others. (9) For you know the grace of our Lord Jesus Christ, that though he was rich, yet for your sakes he became poor, so that you through his poverty might become rich (2 Corinthians 8:1-9).

Vignettes of Giving

The state of blessedness doesn't depend on the amount of money you have.

It's a lesson Miss Oseola McCarty took a lifetime to learn. Not that she ever had much money. She slaved for decades to earn a meager fifty cents a load doing laundry for families in Hattiesburg, Mississippi. Even on that pittance the thrifty lady managed to squirrel away a bit every week in her savings account at the local bank. When she retired, well past the standard retirement age, she got around to asking the banker how much money she had in her account.

"Two hundred fifty thousand dollars," was his reply.

The laundry lady, now in her eighties, was in shock. What was she to do with such an estate? "I had more than I could use in the bank. I can't carry anything away from here with me, so I thought it was best to give it to some child to get an education."

Always self-effacing, the unmarried Miss McCarty had simple needs, but her heart was big. She gave $150,000 to nearby University of Southern Mississippi to help young people attend college. "It's more blessed to give than to receive," she tells reporters. "I've tried it!"

When we worshiped with the Nepalese Christians in Kathmandu . . . more than two hundred believers were there. The service had already stretched to nearly two and a half hours and was coming to a close when the pastor told the congregation of a tragedy that had indirectly struck their church. The son of the man who drove the church's station wagon had fallen off a roof two days earlier and was still in a coma. The father had gone immediately to the distant town to be with his son. Living like most of the Nepalese from day to day, he had no money for the journey or for his son's expenses. Immediately after the pastor told the congregation of the man's plight, he prayed the benediction. The members spontaneously began singing as they left the building—by way of the open sack in front of the pulpit into which they placed their second offering of the morning. These were very poor people, giving and giving again, singing and praising God because they could help someone in need.

Two or three times Sarita, who was sitting across from me at dinner one evening, casually mentioned the people's tithes. Finally I asked, "Sarita, do all the Christians tithe?" "Oh yes," she assured me, then went on at length to tell me how the tithes enabled the church help needy people. These Christians earned no more money than the pittance their neighbors earned, yet they all had enough to care for their own needs and give to others as well.

—excerpted from LeRoy Lawson, *Blessed Are We*

Exploring the Text

2 Corinthians 2:1-9

Who were the Macedonians and why would Paul praise them?

The churches in Macedonia (Philippi, Thessalonica, and Berea) sent funds to the poor saints in Jerusalem even though they themselves were extremely poor. Why? Macedonia suffered economically due to the harsh treatment of the conquering Romans, who had exploited their natural resources. In addition, civil wars had been fought in their area and there had been little opportunity to rebuild. They gave much more than anyone would expect of people in their circumstances. And they gave willingly, not just because they were asked. They also gave themselves to the Lord and put themselves at Paul's disposal (v. 5).

What was Titus's role?

It appears that Titus had previously begun to take a collection of money among the Corinthians, but had been interrupted. Paul planned to send Titus again to complete the collection.

Aren't comparisons wrong (v. 8)?

Paul was holding up the Macedonians as an example and urged the Corinthians to test their sincerity by comparing it to the Macedonians. But he wasn't comparing the Corinthians and Macedonians in the sense of asking who was better. He encouraged his readers, the Corinthians, to be inspired by the example of the Macedonians, as stated so well in this biblical principle: "As iron sharpens iron, so one man sharpens another" (Proverbs 27:17).

Besides, the Corinthians didn't need to be pumped up with a contest or competition. They were well equipped to give by the grace they were given (excellence in faith, speech, knowledge, earnestness, and love, v. 7). With this grace, they could become good givers too.

Good Deeds in Secret

Here is the experience of a woman who lived in a dormitory with other women.

In my early twenties, I had been reading the edited biography of Therese of Lisieux, the "Little Flower," and I was touched and inspired by her hidden way to holiness, her "little way." I decided to do at least one small act of kindness each day that was completely unknown to anyone.

So I would keep my eyes peeled for something helpful I could do that no one would see. I wanted to be absolutely sure that I was doing it for no one but God, whom I loved with a kind of simple and quite passionate fervor. I made the beds. I folded clothes. I tidied. At least one act each day, and no one knew. Now what's important here is that very infinitesimal act each day gave me enormous joy because no one saw it. It gave me a kind of inner excitement to do this only for God: a secret between me and God. It kept me alert to the small needs of others; maybe it provided spontaneity and creativity in an otherwise highly regimented situation.

If you were to follow her lead, what would you do?

1) _____

2) _____

3) _____

4) _____

Twelve

What a Way to Go

When I visited Ray Payne] in the hospital, he had just days to live. Pneumonia was rapidly claiming his life. [A little earlier, he had told his wife Betty he wanted to die.] He was not depressed nor suicidal; he wasn't giving up in despair. He trusted the Lord's grace. He believed his time had come, and he was worn out. More importantly, he was looking ahead.

As we circled [around his bedside for prayer,] I noted that he seemed stronger than . . . just a few minutes earlier. With our hands clasped around the bed, Ray removed his [oxygen] mask and, not waiting for anyone else, prayed vigorously. He didn't ask a thing for himself; his prayer was for us. I was so moved I had difficulty speaking when my turn came. . . . If the Scriptures are to be believed, he was greeted in Heaven by joy. "Welcome to the wedding feast. We're so glad you came." You will be, too.

—LeRoy Lawson, *Blessed Are We*

Central Theme	Death is not to be feared because Heaven will be a place of rest and joy.
Lesson Aim	Group members will look at biblical information on joy and rest in Heaven and explore what it means to believe this.
Bible Background	Isaiah 11:6-9; Hebrews 4:1, 9-11; Revelation 14:13
For Further Study	Read Chapter 12 of *Blessed Are We*.

PLAN ONE

Classes

BUILDING COMMUNITY

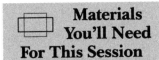

Nine Facts, One Lie
5-10 minutes

Display Transparency 12, "Which One Is Wrong?" and say, **Which fact listed on this transparency is not true?** Let class members ponder the sheet for a few minutes and get their ideas. The answer is 2—Heaven is God's throne and the earth is God's footstool. Here are the references on which the statements are based in case a class member is interested:
1. Matthew 5:18
2. Matthew 5:34
3. Matthew 22:30
4. Luke 12:32, 33
5. Luke 15:10
6. Acts 7:55, 56
7. 2 Corinthians 12:2-4
8. 2 Corinthians 5:1; Hebrews 11:16
9. Revelation 7:9
10. Revelation 7:13-17; Revelation 22:5

Materials You'll Need For This Session

Resource Sheets 12A, 12B, Transparency 12, pens or pencils, chalk and chalkboard, 2 pieces of poster board.

Ask class members to consider this question: **What texture would you compare Heaven to? For example, would it be something soft like cotton, lush like fur, or structured like corduroy?** Encourage them to use their imaginations with this. If certain class members can't think of anything, ask if they agree with one of the other class member's responses.

OPTION
Texture Comparison
8-10 minutes

CONSIDERING SCRIPTURE

Distribute copies of Resource Sheet 12A, "Glimpses of Heaven," and ask class members to form groups of four or five. Read the question at the top of the page aloud and then say, **Work together in your group to decide which words or phrases answer the question, What will Heaven be like? Underline the words and phrases you've chosen.**

Allow groups a few minutes to work and then read the first passage and ask a group for their answers. Then ask if other groups had additional or different answers. Do the same with each section, asking a different group to offer the first responses. Here are some phrases the groups may have underlined:

Scripture Search
10-15 minutes

Revelation 14:13 "Blessed are the dead who die in the Lord," "they will rest from their labor"
Isaiah 11:6-9 "The wolf will live with the lamb"
Revelation 19:6-9 "Let us rejoice and be glad and give him glory!" "Blessed are those who are invited"
Hebrews 4:1 "promise of entering his rest"
Hebrews 4:9-11 "a Sabbath-rest for the people of God," "anyone who enters God's rest also rests from his own work," "make every effort to enter that rest"

OPTION
Ad Brochure
12-15 minutes

Distribute colored paper and colored pens and explain, **Many people say they believe in God, but not as many believe in Heaven or Hell. Let's pretend for a moment that you are a sales agent, assigned to put together an advertisement that will depict what Heaven will be like. For our purposes, focus on the attributes presented in today's Scripture passage.**

Distribute photocopies of Resource Sheet 12A, "Glimpses of Heaven," or write today's Scripture references on the chalkboard. Class members may wish to create a poster advertisement or perhaps a three-panel brochure by folding the paper in thirds. If any class members seem reluctant, encourage them to work in pairs. After allowing class members several moments to work, ask them to share their brochures, explaining them as they like.

TAKING THE NEXT STEP

Graffiti Posters
10-15 minutes

Before class, draw a female stick figure on a large piece of poster board and put this caption under it, "Betty believes." On another piece of poster board, draw a male stick figure and write this caption, "Douglas doubts." Display these two pieces of poster board and then lay them flat on a table or on the floor. Lay several pens or pencils next to them.

Say to class members, **Consider the merits of believing that God provides Heaven for those who believe in Christ. What down-to-earth practical benefits does that provide? What loftier, philosophical benefits does that provide?**

Write your answers to these questions on the "Betty believes" poster. Write graffiti style—sideways, right side up, upside down, any direction you'd like.

After you've done this, consider what the opposite of this benefit would be for those who don't believe. Write that on the "Douglas doubts" poster. Or, write any disadvantage you can think of, even if it's unrelated to the benefit.

When they're finished, hold up each poster board and read the benefits on the "Betty believes" poster. They might include something such as positive attitude toward death, hope for the future, eternal values, focusing on people instead of things. If any of those are not named, you may wish to add them.

OPTION
Continuum
5 minutes

Introduce this portion of the session by distributing photocopies of Resource Sheet 12B, "Explaining the Unexplainable," and draw a horizontal line across the chalkboard. Draw also a midway point. On the left write, "I fully believe." On the right add, "I doubt Heaven exists."

Explain, **Belief and unbelief co-exist within us at times. Sometimes we believe fully in Heaven; other times we tremble in doubt. Draw on the bottom of your sheet this continuum I've drawn on the chalkboard and mark where you are in your belief and doubt.**

OPTION
Sound Reminders
3-5 minutes

Say to class members, **What everyday sounds could we use as reminders that Heaven is real and is part of our future?** They might suggest things such as sirens, or the sound of a rocking chair, or thunder.

Groups

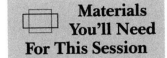

Materials You'll Need For This Session

Reproducible sheet: Resource Sheet 12B.

BUILDING COMMUNITY

1. Ask group members to complete this sentence:

Heaven is a place of _____.

2. What makes you think this is true?

3. What pictures in your imagination do you have of Heaven?

OPTION
Agree/Disagree: Distribute copies of Resource Sheet 12B, "Explaining the Unexplainable," and ask a volunteer to read it aloud. Point out the last statement, "Many of our villagers are already convinced nothing like it exists."

4. Do you agree or disagree? Why?

5. Which of the above tactics has God used in presenting Heaven to people? If necessary, remind class members of quotes from Revelation about streets of gold and gates made of pearls (21:18, 21).

CONSIDERING SCRIPTURE

Read Revelation 14:13.

1. What "beatitude" (phrase of blessedness) do you find in this verse?

2. Why, according to this verse, is the deceased person blessed?

Read Revelation 19:6-9.

3. Who is "blessed" in this passage?

4. Why are these people rejoicing?

Read Isaiah 11:6-9.

OPTION
Accountability Partners
Have accountability partners meet and discuss ways they remind themselves of Heaven and their future. You may want to suggest they come up with "sound reminders" (See Classes session, **Taking the Next Step,** last option.)

OPTION
Worship Ideas
Read Psalm 62 together as an act of worship. Song Suggestions: "Our God Reigns" by Leonard E. Smith; "A Shield About Me" by Donn Thomas & Charles Williams.

OPTION
Memory Verse
Then I heard a voice from heaven say, "Write: Blessed are the dead who die in the Lord from now on." "Yes," says the Spirit, "they will rest from their labor, for their deeds will follow them" (Revelation 14:13).

5. What unusual things will happen in this description of Heaven? (If group members have trouble with this, back up and ask this question: What is the *normal* relationship between a wolf and a lamb, a leopard and a goat, a calf and a lion and a yearling? These are natural enemies—the wolf and leopard and lion are naturally the predators of these other animals.)

6. What do these extraordinary conditions tell us about the atmosphere of Heaven?

Read Hebrews 4:1, 9-11.

7. What promises are mentioned in these verses? (the promise of entering a Sabbath-rest)

8. In what ways is a Sabbath-rest a desirable thing?

9. What do you think the phrase, "make every effort to enter that rest" means? (Make sure group members don't get the impression that this promotes salvation by works. Heaven is a place of being with God forever and nurturing the relationship formed here on earth. Obedience flows out of a well-developed relationship with God.)

TAKING THE NEXT STEP

1. How does a belief in Heaven change our day-to-day approach to life? (If necessary, prod class members further regarding values such as materialism and success. What does it mean about saving up for the future? What does it tell us about what is really valuable?)

2. Practically speaking, how can a belief in Heaven change our day-to-day behavior?

3. What could we do to become more aware of Heaven in our day-to-day life?

Glimpses of Heaven

What will Heaven be like?

Revelation 14:13
Then I heard a voice from heaven say, "Write: Blessed are the dead who die in the Lord from now on." "Yes," says the Spirit, "they will rest from their labor, for their deeds will follow them."

Isaiah 11:6-9
(6) The wolf will live with the lamb, the leopard will lie down with the goat, the calf and the lion and the yearling together; and a little child will lead them. (7) The cow will feed with the bear, their young will lie down together, and the lion will eat straw like the ox. (8) The infant will play near the hole of the cobra, and the young child put his hand into the viper's nest. (9) They will neither harm nor destroy on all my holy mountain, for the earth will be full of the knowledge of the LORD as the waters cover the sea.

Revelation 19:6-9
(6) Then I heard what sounded like a great multitude, like the roar of rushing waters and like loud peals of thunder, shouting: "Hallelujah! For our Lord God Almighty reigns. (7) Let us rejoice and be glad and give him glory! For the wedding of the Lamb has come, and his bride has made herself ready. (8) Fine linen, bright and clean, was given her to wear." (Fine linen stands for the righteous acts of the saints.) (9) Then the angel said to me, "Write: 'Blessed are those who are invited to the wedding supper of the Lamb!'" And he added, "These are the true words of God."

Hebrews 4:1, 9-11
(1) Therefore, since the promise of entering his rest still stands, let us be careful that none of you be found to have fallen short of it. . . . (9) There remains, then, a Sabbath-rest for the people of God; (10) for anyone who enters God's rest also rests from his own work, just as God did from his. (11) Let us, therefore, make every effort to enter that rest, so that no one will fall by following their example of disobedience.

Explaining the Unexplainable

Earlier in this century, a Greenland Eskimo was taken on an American expedition to the North Pole. As a reward for faithful service on the trek, he was brought to New York City for a visit. He had never seen anything like it. The tall buildings piercing the skyline, the little rooms that rose vertically to the top of them, the display windows bursting with garments and furniture and trinkets he had never imagined. He was filled with awe. He could hardly wait to return to his native village, where he told stories of those buildings that rose to the face of the sky and of street cars, which he described as houses that moved along a trail with people living in them as they moved. He told of mammoth bridges, artificial lights, and all the other dazzling phenomena of the great metropolis. His neighbors' response surprised him as much as the city sights had. They stared coldly and walked away. They didn't believe him. What he described was impossible. They dubbed him Sagdluk, "the liar." In time, they even forgot his original name. He was known—to his shame—as "The Liar" until he died.

When Knud Rasmussen undertook his expedition from Greenland to Alaska he took along an Eskimo named Mitek, "Elder Duck." Mitek visited Copenhagen and New York; his discoveries closely paralleled Sagdluk's, whose tragedy he remembered. He decided it would be to his advantage not to tell the whole truth. He told only stories that his people could grasp. He described how he and Dr. Rasmussen maintained a Kayak on the banks of a great river, and how each morning they paddled out for their hunting. Most of his adventures he kept to himself. In the eyes of his countrymen, Mitek was a very honest man. His neighbors treated him with rare respect.

How, then, shall we talk about Heaven? Many of our villagers are already convinced nothing like it exists.

—excerpted from LeRoy Lawson, *Blessed Are We*

Which One Is Wrong?

One of these ten statements is not true, according to Scripture. Can you figure out which one it is?

1. Heaven will disappear.

2. Heaven is God's footstool.

3. In Heaven, people won't marry; they'll be like angels.

4. In Heaven, what you have is thief-proof.

5. Angels have a party (rejoice) whenever anyone repents.

6. Before Stephen (the martyr whose death is recorded in Acts) died, he got to look up to Heaven, see God's glory, and see Jesus standing at the right hand of God.

7. Paul spoke of a man who had been caught up in Heaven and heard inexpressible things that he wasn't allowed to talk about.

8. Christians not only have an eternal house prepared for them in Heaven but an entire city.

9. Someone from every nation will be present in Heaven.

10. In Heaven, God will wipe every tear from our eyes and there will be no more night.

Thirteen

The Blessings of Belief

*I*s doubting a sin or does doubt shut down] the power that faith releases? Did Peter sin when, walking on the water, he turned his eyes from Jesus to the waves and began to sink? Wasn't it rather that he wavered, lost his "grip" and thus his power? Jesus immediately reached out his hand and caught him. "You of little faith," he said, "why did you doubt?" (Matthew 4:31). It is a bit of a scolding, all right. But for this momentary lapse Jesus doesn't banish Peter from his company. His point is more basic: When you were trusting me and walking by faith, you were doing something extraordinary.

God doesn't expect us to stop thinking when we become Christians, or to forget the lessons, sometimes bitter, that life has taught us. . . . Without entertaining other possibilities, including the refusal to believe, belief is rendered meaningless. . . . As Philip Toynbee pointed out near the end of his spiritual journey, "How very few holy persons have combined deep spiritual passion with openness of mind and heart. We must try to do both."

—LeRoy Lawson, *Blessed Are We*

Central Theme   Belief in God (and working through the doubts involved) blesses us by giving us a confident independence from our culture, and an assurance of our future.

Lesson Aim   Group members will look at a biblical example of doubt resolved, and explore the benefits of an honest, open-minded belief.

Bible Background   Matthew 11:1-6; John 20:29

For Further Study   Read Chapter 13 of *Blessed Are We.*

Classes

BUILDING COMMUNITY

Write the following statement on the chalkboard or say it a few times: "Doubt can help your faith." Then ask, **Do you agree or disagree with this statement?** Ask one or two people who agree to explain their reason; then do the same with the other side. If too many members are on one side or the other, goad those in the majority with these opposite ideas:

Say to those who agree: **Didn't Jesus say, "I tell you the truth, if anyone says to this mountain, 'Go, throw yourself into the sea,' and does not doubt in his heart but believes that what he says will happen, it will be done for him"** (Mark 11:23)?

Say to those who disagree: **The father of the demon-possessed boy openly admitted his unbelief, but Jesus healed his son anyway** (Mark 9:24).

Keep in mind that at this point your goal is to raise questions, not to answer them. Don't rush in with answers, but let the curiosity (or even frustration) of class members draw them into the lesson.

Use the same agree-disagree activity, but make it more active for class members who respond well to activity. Have those who agree stand on one side of the room and those who disagree stand on the other.

CONSIDERING SCRIPTURE

Distribute paper and pencils and have group members read John 20:29. Display Resource Sheet 13A, "Page Torn From a Commentary," and read the Scripture in the left column together. Explain, **A commentary is a reference book that comments on Scripture and gives us clues from the context that help us understand the passage. Here are some comments by Dr. LeRoy Lawson, printed as if they were torn from a page in a commentary.**

Then ask a class member to read the right column "commentary." Ask, **Do you agree with this interpretation of John the Baptist's behavior—which is full of doubt—and Jesus' response?**

Then distribute pencils and copies of Resource Sheet 13B,

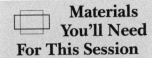

Agree-Disagree
5-10 minutes

Materials You'll Need For This Session

Resource Sheets 13A, 13B, Transparency 13, pens or pencils, chalk and chalkboard, cassette recorder and blank cassette for each small group (optional).

Stand Out
5-10 minutes

Journal Entries
10-15 minutes

"What Would You Have Written?" Divide the class into two groups. Read the instructions at the top aloud and say, **Imagine for a moment that you are John the Baptist as portrayed in Matthew 11:1-3. Write an imaginary entry in his journal. Feel free to express his doubts and questions and how he plans to send his disciples as agents to discover the truth.** Assign this to the first group. Ask the second group to do the same with the lower portion—Jesus' reply to John.

OPTION
Last Telephone Call
10-15 minutes

Have the class form pairs with one class member playing the role of John the Baptist and another playing the role of Jesus. Use the material from Resource Sheet 13A, "Page Torn From a Commentary," if you wish. Then explain, **Work with a partner, with one partner assuming the role of John the Baptist and the other Jesus. Then put together an imaginary last telephone call in which John expresses the doubts he expressed in this passage. The partner who assumes the role of Jesus should respond as it seems to him that Jesus responded.** If you have time, have one or two pairs come to the front and present the imaginary telephone call they just put together.

OPTION
Taped Thoughts
10-15 minutes

Have the class form small groups and introduce the passage as stated above. Use the material from Resource Sheet 13A, "Page Torn From a Commentary," if you wish. Give these instructions: **First, consider what John the Baptist was thinking as the events recorded in verses 1-3 occurred. Have one person in your group jot those down. Then consider the same for Jesus in the events of verses 4-6. Have the same person jot these down.** Allow them time to do this.

Then give each group a cassette tape recorder and blank tape. **Choose one person from your group to record the thoughts of John and another to record the thoughts of Jesus. Both should work from the notes you've put together.** Reconvene the groups and play the taped thoughts for the entire group.

TAKING THE NEXT STEP

Group Discussion
10-15 minutes

Distribute copies of Transparency 13, "Blessings of Belief," and ask a volunteer to read it aloud. After each category is read, stop and ask the class this question: **What specific blessings flow out of belief?** For example, the first two combine to show us how important it is to love people and use things instead of loving things and using people.

OPTION
Paper Tear
5-7 minutes

Distribute small pieces of paper (for example, cut 8 1/2 x 11 sheets of paper into quarters). After you've finished the above discussion (or in place of it), say to class members, **Tear this sheet into the shape of an object that somehow relates to a blessing that comes from your belief. For example, with the idea of escaping materialism, someone might tear his sheet into a dollar sign.** (For fun, you could keep track of which class member was the first to arrive, and give that person scissors!)

Distribute copies of Transparency 13, "Blessings of Belief," and ask a volunteer to read it aloud. Then ask, **How do you think John the Baptist's questions and expression of doubts could have fostered the blessings on this page?** Point out, if necessary, that John was going to die and this airing of doubts probably fostered a confidence and assurance he would desperately need.

OPTION
Researching John the Baptist's Blessings
5-7 minutes

Groups

BUILDING COMMUNITY

Read this quote or write it on the chalkboard: **How very few holy persons have combined deep spiritual passion with openness of mind and heart. We must try to do both.**

1. Why is it easy for a deeply spiritual person to have a closed mind and heart?

2. What sort of open-mindedness does a person with "deep spiritual passion" need to have?

3. What sort of open-heartedness does a person with "deep spiritual passion" need to have?

Encourage group members to share their experiences because their experiences may explain their answers better than anything else.

CONSIDERING SCRIPTURE

Read John 20:29.

Introduce these verses by saying, **These words were spoken by Jesus after Thomas said he wouldn't believe that Jesus had raised from the dead until he could touch his wounds.**

1. What could Jesus have possibly meant by an additional blessing being given to those who believed without seeing?

Read Matthew 11:1-3.

2. What do we already know about John the Baptist? (John had already identified Jesus as the Messiah by this time, John 1:29, 36)

3. In light of John's previous faith, why did his question (v. 3) seem odd?

4. What might have precipitated this question from John?

Read Matthew 11:4-6.

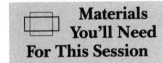

Materials You'll Need For This Session

Reproducible sheet:
Transparency 13.

5. Why was Jesus' answer appropriate? (If necessary, mention that he quoted Isaiah 6:1, 2, a prophecy of the Messiah.)

6. How did quoting Isaiah 6:1, 2 give John greater reason to believe Jesus was the Messiah? (Fulfilled prophecy is a great proof of the truth of Scripture and the truth that Jesus was the Messiah. As a prophet, John the Baptist would have been especially sensitive to this and respected that proof.)

7. Why do you think Jesus included his comment in verse 6? (If necessary, follow up with, Who was Jesus talking about? It would appear to be John. Jesus was expressing confidence John would find tremendous blessing, not fall away, and sense that his faith was restored.)

TAKING THE NEXT STEP

Display Transparency 13, "Blessings of Belief," or make photocopies of it for group members.

1. What blessings have you experienced because your faith hasn't allowed you to fall for just anything?

2. What blessings have you experienced because your faith has helped you see the big picture?

3. What blessings have you experienced because your faith has helped you align yourself with God's side—the "right side"?

4. What blessings have you experienced because your faith has given you greater confidence and assurance?

Blessings of Belief

Blessing: You Don't Fall for Just Anything

Was it G.K. Chesterton who warned that the problem with banishing God from your life is not that you now believe in nothing, but that you may fall for anything? . . . Some people are pretty serious about Elvis. George Reiger, whose body features 303 Disney-related tattoos says, "This is my religion. This is my life. Every cent I have goes to Disney."

Blessing: Being Able to See the Big Picture

My experience with genuine believers has left me marveling at the depth of their understanding, the breadth of their perspective. They live in a big world; it encompasses all reality, limited by neither time nor space. They are no longer trapped by illusions, rationalizations, prejudices, and attachments.

Blessing: Being on the Right Side

"A religion is, at its heart, a way of denying the authority of the rest of the world; it is a way of saying to fellow human beings and to the state those fellow humans have erected, 'No, I will not accede to your will.'"

Blessing: Blessed Assurance

Our blessed assurance is that the last word is "a living hope through the resurrection of Jesus Christ from the dead, and into an inheritance that can never perish, spoil or fade—kept in heaven" for us (1 Peter 1:3, 4).

—adapted from LeRoy Lawson, *Blessed Are We*

Page Torn From a Commentary

MATTHEW 11

JOHN THE BAPTIST'S QUESTION

(1) After Jesus had finished instructing his twelve disciples, he went on from there to teach and preach in the towns of Galilee. (2) When John heard in prison what Christ was doing, he sent his disciples (3) to ask him, "Are you the one who was to come, or should we expect someone else?"

JESUS' RESPONSE

(4) Jesus replied, "Go back and report to John what you hear and see: (5) The blind receive sight, the lame walk, those who have leprosy are cured, the deaf hear, the dead are raised, and the good news is preached to the poor. (6) Blessed is the man who does not fall away on account of me."

Commentary
(thanks to Dr. LeRoy Lawson, *Blessed Are We*)

(vv. 1-3) In the Scriptures even a prophet like John the Baptist had his moments of doubt. From his prison cell he dispatches his disciples to check Jesus out. This is the same man who baptized Jesus, who called him the "Lamb of God, who takes away the sin of the world." But that was then, and now, as he languished in prison, John hesitated. He wondered, "Could I have been wrong? Why didn't he rescue me? Did I promote a fraud?" Perhaps he heard gossip from Herod's guards about Jesus being in trouble with the authorities.

(vv. 4-6) Jesus doesn't take offense. He sends John's messengers back with a direct reply about Isaiah's messianic prophecy being fulfilled. "Look at my ministry, then compare it with Isaiah 61:1, 2, and you will see I am fulfilling the job description of the promised one."

FYI: Isaiah 61:1, 2: The Spirit of the Sovereign Lord is on me, because the Lord has anointed me to preach good news to the poor. He has sent me to bind up the brokenhearted, to proclaim freedom for the captives and release from darkness for the prisoners, to proclaim the year of the Lord's favor and the day of vengeance of our God, to comfort all who mourn. . . .

What Would You Have Written?

Read Matthew 11:1-3.
What do you think John the Baptist might have written in a private journal?

Read Matthew 3:4-6.
From this passage, we know Jesus' public response to his cousin's doubts.
What do you think Jesus might have written in his journal?

Other Creative Groups Guides
from Standard Publishing

PRAISE UNDER PRESSURE

13 lessons by David Faust, Troy Jackson
Study the life of King David to learn how to cope with life's pressures.
Order number 40320 (ISBN 0-7847-0490-2)

THE NEW TESTAMENT CHURCH THEN AND NOW

13 lessons by Timothy Heck
Equip yourselves to continue the mission as the first-century church.
Order number 40322 (ISBN 0-7847-0492-9)

DREAM INTRUDERS

6 lessons by Tim Sutherland
Find ways to overcome difficult times and temporary setbacks in life.
Order number 40312 (ISBN 0-7847-0392-2)

FIND US FAITHFUL

13 lessons by Michael D. McCann
Learn to pass on your faith to the next generation.
Order number 40308 (ISBN 0-7847-0308-6)

FAITH'S FUNDAMENTALS

7 lessons by Kent C. Odor, Mark Ingmire
Equip yourselves with the seven essentials of Christian belief.
Order number 40311 (ISBN 0-7847-0391-4)

LIFE PRESERVERS

13 lessons by Jan Johnson
Discover ways to rely fully on God's promises.
Order number 40324 (ISBN 0-7847-0574-7)

CARRY ON!

13 lessons by Timothy Heck
Find help and hope for life's everyday battles.
Order number 40316 (ISBN 0-7847-0486-4)

VICTORY IN JESUS

13 lessons by Jan Johnson
Learn to live victoriously in your life in Christ.
Order number 40314 (ISBN 0-7847-0424-4)

A CALL TO PRAYER

7 lessons by Jan Johnson
Learn to pray effectively, sincerely, with power, and without hindrances.
Order number 40309 (ISBN 0-7847-0309-4)

CLAIMING YOUR PLACE

7 lessons by Michael C. Mack, Mark A. Taylor
Discover where you fit in the life of the church.
Order number 40305 (ISBN 0-7847-0285-3)

HEARING GOD

6 lessons by Michael C. Mack, Mark A. Taylor
Discover ways to read God's Word—and really understand it!
Order number 40306 (ISBN 0-7847-0286-1)

TAKE COMFORT

13 lessons by Wes Haystead
Find encouragement to remain faithful.
Order number 40325 (ISBN 0-7847-0575-5)

FAITH UNDER FIRE

13 lessons by David Faust, Troy Jackson
Find encouragement to live by faith.
Order number 40328 (ISBN 0-7847-0638-7)

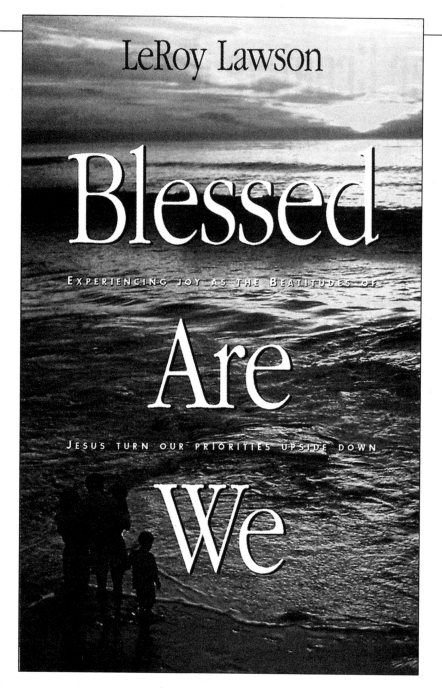